English Revision

Steven Croft

Contents

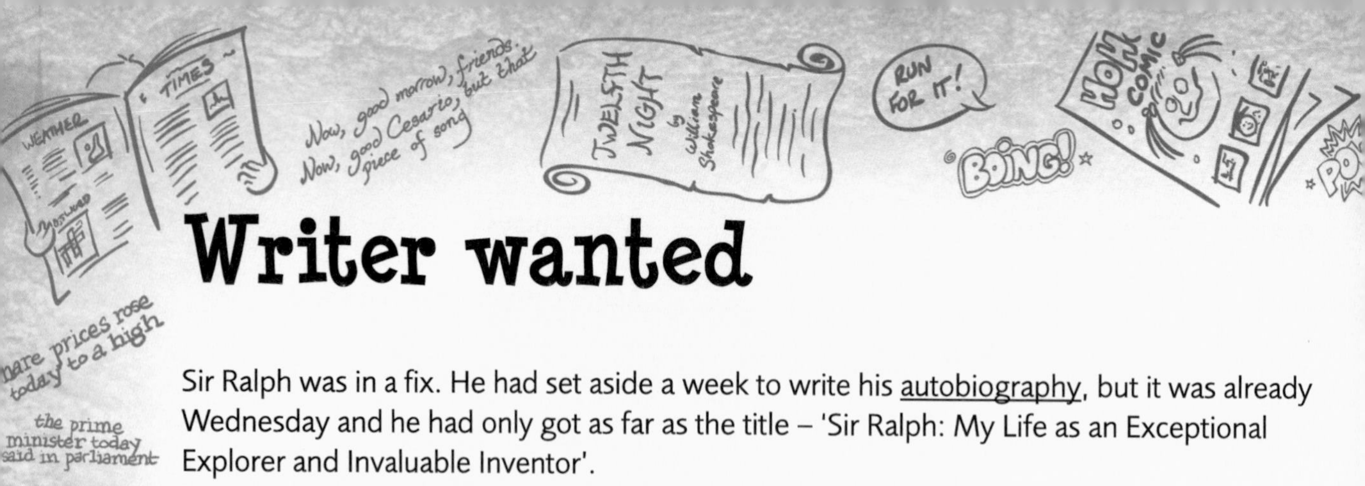

Writer wanted

Sir Ralph was in a fix. He had set aside a week to write his autobiography, but it was already Wednesday and he had only got as far as the title – 'Sir Ralph: My Life as an Exceptional Explorer and Invaluable Inventor'.

The trouble was that he was too much a man of action to be bothered to sit behind a desk for hours on end. He would get an idea for a new invention and rush off to his workshop. Or he would start planning his expedition to Outer Mongolia.

Izzy, Ralph's daughter, suggested that he advertise for a writer to help him, and he reluctantly agreed. 'WRITER WANTED – apply 0354 758494' was all the advert said. Ralph was a man of few words.

On Friday there was a long queue of men and women outside Ralph's study. They had all come for the job.

'What newspaper do you run?' asked the first. 'I'm a journalist.'

'Who is it that you want to write to?' asked the second. 'I'm a secretary.'

'What story are you trying to write?' asked the third. 'I'm a novelist.'

'What is it that you want to sell?' asked the fourth. 'I write adverts.'

'What is it that you want people to do?' asked the fifth. 'I write instruction manuals.'

'Get out!' yelled Ralph. 'Get out, get out, get out, get out!'

'Perhaps you should have specified that you wanted help with your autobiography, Sir,' muttered Max the housekeeper, as he showed them all the door.

Ralph scowled. He put a line through the title of his book and turned to the map of Outer Mongolia.

What kind of writing?

You work for a busy media company. Various kinds of writing have arrived in the post. Your job is to put them in the correct pigeonhole. For example, if you think the 'Life of Shakespeare' is a magazine, draw an arrow linking it with the pigeonhole labelled 'magazines'.

• TOP TIPS •

- Look at the different kinds of writing you see around you every day and think about which category each fits into.
- When writing anything, or analysing a text, you need to know what its purpose is and what audience it is aimed at.
- Fiction is writing that comes out of the writer's imagination. Non-fiction deals with facts.

DID YOU KNOW?

Did you know that the average daily newspaper often contains more than 20 different types of writing, e.g. reports, horoscopes, problem pages, film and TV reviews, adverts.

A useful invention

Ralph was in another one of his moods. He had just received a telephone call from the 'Clever Stuff Company', which specialises in selling new and unusual inventions. The company told him that they did not want his new invention – a foldable bicycle that was so light and small it would fit into a sports bag.

'I simply don't understand it, Max,' he said to his housekeeper. 'These days, when we are so concerned with energy conservation, global warming and health and fitness I thought they would have snapped up my invention.'

'It does seem hard to understand,' replied Max, diplomatically.

'It isn't at all hard to understand,' broke in Izzy, who had overheard the conversation. I watched you sending off the package to 'Clever Stuff Company'. You put your bike in, sure, but there was no proper letter with it arguing why it's such a good invention. There was just a scrappy note saying, 'My latest brainwave – photos of me cycling up the Alps will follow when I find my camera.''

'So what do you suggest I do?' asked her father sheepishly.

'You need to start off by telling them **exactly what you are doing**,' said Izzy. 'Then put all your points down clearly, and in a **logical order**. Make it sound reasonable. Write in **formal English** too – none of your wacky phrases, please.'

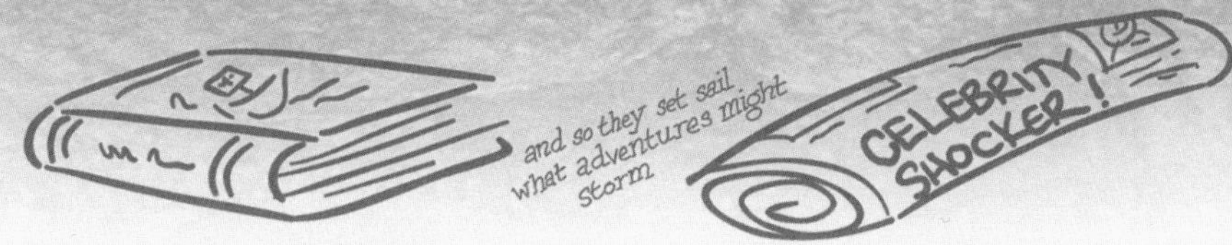

Out of order

Here are some sentences written by someone arguing that their collapsible bike is a good invention. The writer needs help sorting them out so that they are in a logical order. Put a number from 1 to 8 next to each sentence, showing the most effective order for an argument text.

In addition, this cycle is so light and easy to fold away that it can be carried in a sports bag.

There are several reasons why this is a useful invention.

I am writing to you about my idea for a collapsible bicycle.

Please contact me if you require any further information.

Secondly, if more people cycle, pollution will be reduced.

First, by encouraging people to cycle, we are helping the health of the nation.

I would be grateful if you would consider these obvious benefits, and think about manufacturing and selling the bicycle.

This fact will encourage people to use it to get to work or the shops, not just for recreation.

DID YOU KNOW?

The word 'argue' comes from the Latin word *arguere* which means 'to make clear' or 'to accuse'.

How were these meanings connected? Well, if you were accusing someone in a law court, you had to produce a very clear and logical argument!

• TOP TIPS •

In an argument text:

- **your opening sentence or paragraph should clearly state your purpose and viewpoint**
- **your points should be written in a logical order**
- **you should use formal language and a reasonable tone.**

It takes a bit of persuasion

Izzy was getting more and more frustrated with her computer. 'It's so *slow*,' she complained to her father. 'And it just can't do what my friends' computers can do. Let's face it – I've had it three years and it's an antique.'

But persuading Sir Ralph to buy a new computer was as difficult as persuading him to drive to the village shop. Izzy had seen her dad's 'improvements' to equipment before. She knew that he would much rather take the computer to pieces and attempt to insert all the things she was missing – new software, new hardware and even some new ware that was neither soft not hard that he had lying around his workshop.

'You know it will end in disaster, Dad,' she told him. 'Remember when you tried to mend the lawnmower?'

Ralph eventually gave in. He realised that his daughter was right. He asked her to design a really persuasive advert that would guarantee the sale of the old computer for as much money as possible.

'Use every **persuasive technique** in the book,' he said. 'And then try to get Max to give you a lift to the newspaper office in town.'
And off he went.

'What a lot of persuasion it takes to get anything done round here,' thought Izzy as she sat down to compose her advert.

Persuasive crossword

The sentences below give you some statements and advice on how to write persuasively. However, there is a word missing in each sentence. Find the missing word and write it in the space in the crossword.

To help you, all the missing words are given below (out of order).

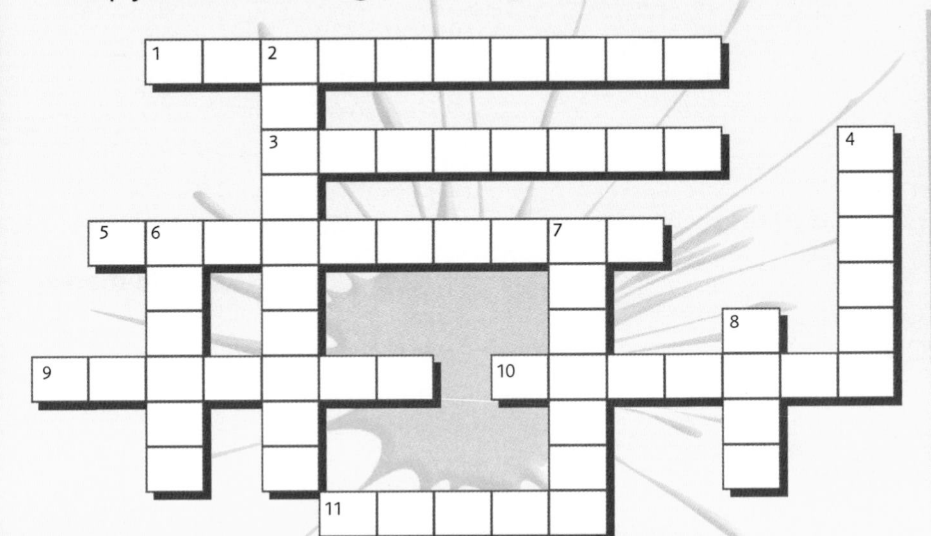

TONE
HUMOUR
RHETORICAL
EMOTIVE
REASONS
ADVERBS
PERSUASIVE
IDEAS
REPETITION
POINTS
PERSONAL

Across

1 Use ……………… techniques.
3 Using the first and second person ('I', 'we' and 'you') is called ……. language.
5 A ……….. question is one that is made for effect – it doesn't expect an answer.
9 ……. language is designed to make the audience feel something.
10 Give clear ……….. for your views.
11 Plan your ……. carefully.

Down

2 ………….. adds emphasis.
4 List all your ………..
6 Using ……. often gets the audience on your side.
7 ……………… add emphasis.
8 Select your …………….. carefully to suit the audience.

• TOP TIPS •

All these techniques can make your language more persuasive:

- **rhetorical questions, e.g. 'What's stopping you?'**
- **repetition, e.g. 'Try, try and try again.'**
- **emotive language, e.g. 'Vote for peace and freedom.'**
- **humour, to get the audience on your side.**

DID YOU KNOW?

One of the longest running advertisements on British TV tried to persuade people to drink a particular type of tea. The PG Tips tea campaign, starring chimpanzees, began in December 1956, when commercial TV in Britain was only in its second year. Over the next 42 years more than 100 different adverts were made. The final one was made in 1994.

Test your knowledge 1

1 Give six examples of different kinds of writing.

a) ....

b) ....

c) ....

d) ....

e) ....

f) ....

(6 marks)

2 a) What is FICTION?

....

b) What is NON-FICTION?

....

(2 marks)

3 The box below lists different types of writing. Underline the ones that are fiction and put a circle round the ones that are non-fiction.

novel	football report	play	short story	biography
history text book	newspaper report	narrative poem		

(8 marks)

4 Explain the following features that you might find in a persuasive piece of writing:

a) bias ....

b) emotive language ....

c) rhetorical question ....

(6 marks)

5 What is the difference between FACTS and OPINIONS?

....

(1 mark)

6 Put an F against the statements below that are facts. Put an O against those that are opinions.

a) Skateboarding is fun.

b) We do not usually go to school on a Sunday.

c) It will rain tomorrow.

d) The Harry Potter novels are really good.

e) 'Pop Idol' is a television programme.

f) English is a brilliant subject.

g) Shakespeare wrote plays.

h) Plays are performed in theatres.

(8 marks)

7 Why might you use repetition when writing an argument?

....

....

(2 marks)

8 Give two examples of writing that puts forward an argument.

a) ....

a) ....

(2 marks)

(Total 35 marks)

Need any help?

One of the highlights of the year for Mrs James, a teacher at Izzy's school, was to organise the weekend visit to a field centre in the Peak District for students in Years 7 and 8. Since Izzy was so keen on hiking and exploring new places, Mrs James asked her to help by writing a leaflet for students, giving information and advice about the trip.

Izzy wanted to be sure that she covered everything before giving the leaflet to Mrs James, so she asked her father for help. She found him in his study.

'Here's just the thing, Izzy,' he said immediately. 'This is a leaflet that I prepared last year for an expedition just like yours. The equipment required was a bit different, of course – we needed sun helmets, anti-cobra bite vaccine, water purifiers, mosquito nets and all kinds of things like that. Not sure you'll want those. You might get some ideas from the **layout** and the **organisation** of the points, though.'

'Thanks, Dad,' said Izzy. She smiled ruefully as she thought of the chaos that can occur when you give the wrong kind of information or advice.

Amazonian Explorers Society

Equipment required

Each member of the expedition will need the following essential items:

- machete
- stout boots
- mosquito net
- water purifying tablets
- waterproof socks
- tropical shorts
- bush hat
- snake bite vaccine
- water bottle
- first aid kit

Advise, inform or explain?

The following material aims to either advise, inform or explain. Tick the category box that best fits its purpose.

		ADVISE	INFORM	EXPLAIN
1	A leaflet giving tips on pet care	☐	☐	☐
2	An instruction booklet on setting up a computer	☐	☐	☐
3	A mobile phone instruction book	☐	☐	☐
4	A bus timetable	☐	☐	☐
5	A guide book about a museum	☐	☐	☐
6	A leaflet about avoiding fires in the home	☐	☐	☐
7	A recipe	☐	☐	☐
8	A leaflet about crossing the road safely	☐	☐	☐
9	A booklet describing the history of your local town	☐	☐	☐
10	A set of directions about how to get to your local sports centre	☐	☐	☐

• TOP TIP •

When writing advice:

- **make your points clear and simple**
- **refer to the reader directly, using 'you' and 'your'**
- **use bullet points and other devices to present the advice clearly.**

DID YOU KNOW?

You can get advice on almost anything from the internet, such as road safety for cyclists or caring for pets.

A novel approach

One rainy day, Sir Ralph felt a sudden urge to try his hand at writing a novel. 'As you know, Max,' he said airily to his housekeeper, 'I've been writing books for years. But all my writing so far has been about inventions, exploration and so on.'

'Yes, Sir Ralph, I know what you mean – you are very good at writing non-fiction.'

'That's true, Max, and now feel I want to have a shot at writing imaginatively. It shouldn't be too difficult. After all, writing's writing. It all uses words.'

Max looked a little doubtful. 'Yes, but writing a novel requires quite a different approach, if you don't mind me saying so, Sir. You need to think of a plot, for example.'

'And good characters,' piped up Izzy, who happened to be passing.

'And a realistic setting,' went on Max, now encouraged by having Izzy as an ally.

'And use words and images in a powerful and imaginative way,' added Izzy.

Ralph's head was turning from one to the other as they spoke. 'Now that's quite enough of telling me what to do. You'll be the characters in my story, if you're not careful, and you may not like the plot!'

'So what *is* the plot, Daddy dear?' teased Izzy.

'It's a mystery story,' barked Ralph, 'so how should I know?'

Where's that word?

Unscramble the following anagrams to find ten words that are all linked in some way with imaginative and descriptive writing.

1 **noctfii** ....

2 **idetcjaev** ....

3 lenvo ....

4 bedarv ....

5 **lbayucorva** ....

6 **yymtsre** ....

7 **santfya** ....

8 nitaco ....

9 iratanrev ....

10 **hotsr ytosr** ....

• TOP TIP •

To write a successful story you need to:

- **plan your plot (storyline) carefully**
- **capture and maintain your reader's interest**
- **use powerful vocabulary and imagery**
- **include dialogue.**

DID YOU KNOW?

Joanne Kathleen Rowling was only six when she wrote her first book. Twenty years later she wrote the first of her Harry Potter novels. This was rejected by several publishers before she finally found one who bought it for a small amount. By the year 2000, the first three Harry Potter books had sold over 35 million copies and had been translated into 35 languages, making JK Rowling a multi-millionaire and one of Britain's wealthiest women.

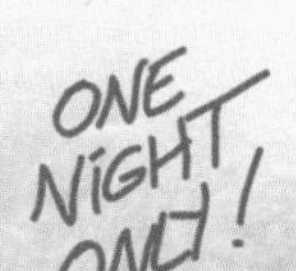

the wizard stared at the enormous fire-breathing dragon and said

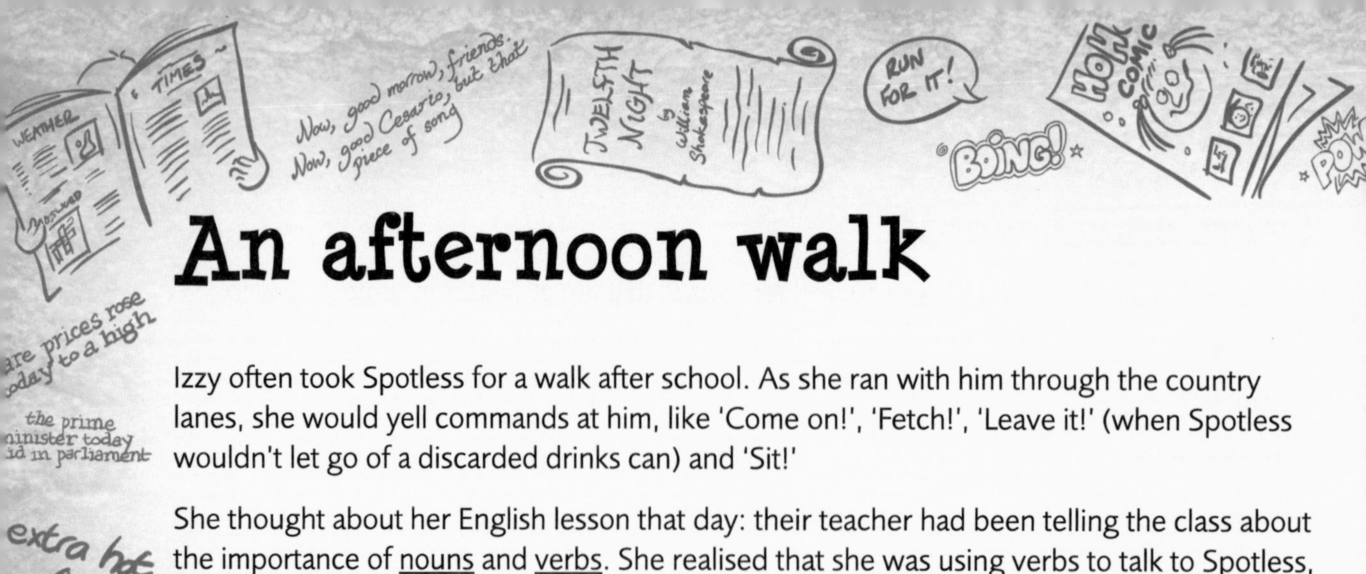

An afternoon walk

Izzy often took Spotless for a walk after school. As she ran with him through the country lanes, she would yell commands at him, like 'Come on!', 'Fetch!', 'Leave it!' (when Spotless wouldn't let go of a discarded drinks can) and 'Sit!'

She thought about her English lesson that day: their teacher had been telling the class about the importance of nouns and verbs. She realised that she was using verbs to talk to Spotless, because verbs were 'doing' words. 'You are such an active dog,' she thought out loud, 'that you only understand verbs.'

Spotless wondered about this as he trotted beside his mistress. He thought she had only half the picture, as there were lots of nouns in his life too. There were proper nouns, such as 'Izzy' and indeed his own name, 'Spotless'. There were common nouns like 'cat' (to be chased) and collective nouns, such as 'flock' (not to be chased). There were even abstract nouns, such as 'a sleep' and 'happiness', which generally went together after a long afternoon's walk.

Complete the spiral

Look at the clues below. The last letter of each answer is the first letter of the next. Link the words to complete the spiral.

1 Verb – faster than walk

2 Noun – six is one of these

3 Noun – opposite to left

4 Verb – to put something on your tongue

5 Noun – you use these to listen

6 Noun – something you can sit on

7 Verb – you might fall over if you...

8 Verb – you might do this for fun

9 Noun – a kind of sailing boat

10 Noun – a kind of dance

11 Noun – a kind of fruit

12 Verb – what you do when hungry

13 Noun – you take this camping

14 Verb – to solve a puzzle you need to...

15 Noun – a unit of weight

16 Verb – to shift something

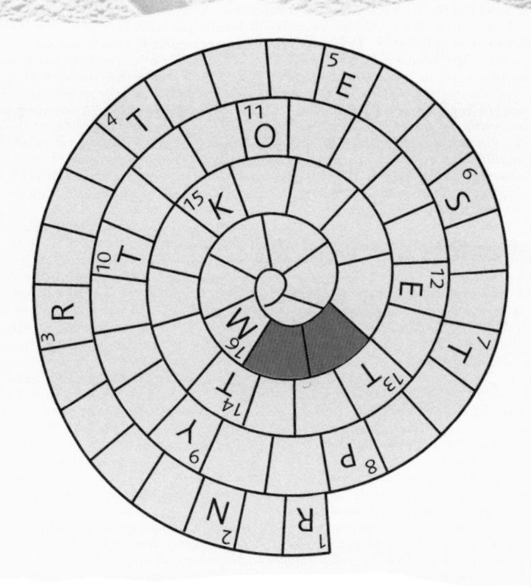

TOP TIP

Nouns are words that name objects or qualities. There are several different types of nouns, such as:

- **proper nouns – these name people and places, e.g. Bill, Birmingham. They have capital letters.**
- **common nouns – these name ordinary things, e.g. blackbird, bone. They don't have capital letters.**

DID YOU KNOW?

Although most sentences contain both a subject (noun) and a verb, many of the sentences that we see around us do not.

- **Keep Left**
- **Exit**
- **The new T630 with Quickshare.**

These are called *special sentences*.

Test your knowledge 2

1 List FOUR types of text that might present advice to the reader. For example: a leaflet on caring for a pet.

a) ....

b) ....

c) ....

d) ....

(4 marks)

2 Fill in the missing words:

a) When writing an advice leaflet, your information should be c _ _ _ _ and c _ _ c_ _ e.

b) It should be divided into clear s _ _ t _ _ n _ _ _.

c) You might use b _ _ _ _ t points to present the ideas clearly.

d) You should be clear about your target a _ d _ _ _ c _ and your p _ _ p _ _ _.

(6 marks)

3 Write down THREE things that an effective story might contain.

a) an effective p ....

b) convincing c ....

c) an interesting s ....

(3 marks)

4 What should the opening of a good story do?

....

(1 mark)

5 What is meant by the 'PLOT' of a story?

....

(1 mark)

6 What is the 'SETTING' of a story?

....

(1 mark)

7 How do we learn about characters when we read a story?

a) Through what they ....

b) And what they ....

c) And what others ....

(3 marks)

8 What is a NOUN?

....

(2 marks)

9 In the box of nouns below, underline the PROPER nouns, put a circle round the COMMON nouns, and cross through the ABSTRACT nouns.

fashion
Wednesday
compact disc
Kieran
weight
Manchester
skin
joke
hammer

(9 marks)

10 Underline the correct form of the verb in each of these sentences.

a) It weren't/wasn't my fault.

b) We is/are having a good time.

c) They do/does argue a lot.

d) I has/have finished my homework.

e) I is/am happy about that.

(5 marks)

(Total 35 marks)

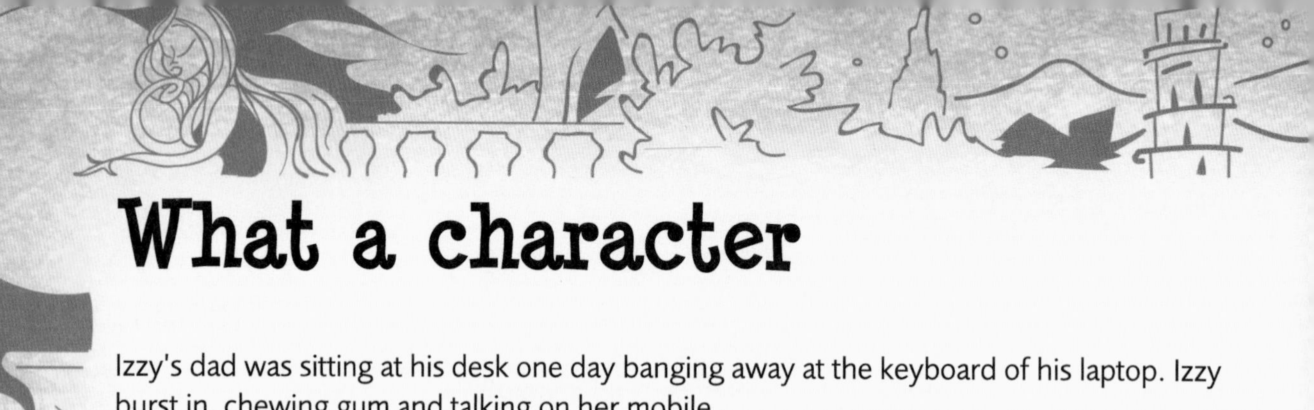

What a character

Izzy's dad was sitting at his desk one day banging away at the keyboard of his laptop. Izzy burst in, chewing gum and talking on her mobile.

'How's your novel coming along Dad?' she said at last.

'Hmmm, I've got the plot planned out but I'm having a bit of trouble creating believable characters. Any ideas?'

'I have, as it happens,' replied Izzy triumphantly. 'In English the other day, Mr Hardcastle told us that it can be useful to get ideas for characters from people we have met or seen.'

'You mean just write about real people?'

'No, silly – **use ideas from your own experience** of people, but create new characters from them.'

'Sounds good.' Ralph looked encouraged. 'Any other bright ideas?'

'Well,' said Izzy, 'you should give your characters names and fill in some background for them, such as age and occupation. You should **avoid stereotypes** too – try to make your characters **convincing**.'

Ralph looked quizzically at his daughter. 'So the teenager who runs up huge phone bills and is in bed half the weekend has to go?'

All about characters

Use the clues to find the missing words.

1							A	**C**								
2							T	**H**								
3					B			**A**	V							
4				D				**R**		P						
5						D		**A**								
6		C	O	N				**C**		N						
7				R		L		**T**			N				P	
8	L			G			G	**E**								
9							C	**R**			T					
10								**S**								

1 The things that characters do.

2 Sometimes the writer reveals what is in a character's mind – what a character ....

3 You learn about characters by how they ....

4 Vivid .... can help you visualise characters.

5 Another word for speech.

6 Characters are this if they appear real.

7 Writers make characters develop .... with other characters.

8 Writers use .... to present their characters.

9 Characters are .... by the writer.

10 Characters are often revealed by what they ....

• TOP TIP •

When creating your characters:

- **picture the people clearly in your head**
- **base your characters on real people, but mix up the features of people you know**
- **give details of their clothes, physical appearance etc. to make them real**
- **don't create stereotypes, if you want your story to be realistic.**

DID YOU KNOW?

HG Wells' story *War of the Worlds* was so convincing that when it was read on the radio in America some people thought the Martians had really invaded Earth. Hundreds of people fled from their homes in New York and New Jersey.

I've got a funny feeling about this place...

Ralph, Izzy and Max decided to visit a ruined manor house a few miles from their home. It was late in the afternoon when they arrived, so they found themselves exploring the grounds at dusk.

'You know this castle is supposed to be haunted?' said Ralph.

'I can believe that!' said Izzy. 'It feels really creepy.'

'You're right,' said Max, appearing out of the gloom. 'I think this would make an excellent setting for a ghost story.'

'Ah, setting and atmosphere!' broke in Sir Ralph – so suddenly that Izzy jumped in fright. '**Setting and atmosphere** are two things I've got to have in my novel. They are really important in writing a good story, you know.'

Max smiled to himself. It was he that had told Ralph in the first place.

'What do you mean, Dad?' asked Izzy.

Ralph closed his eyes and began speaking. 'It's quite simple really. The setting is just the name we give for the *place* a story is set in. The atmosphere is the kind of *feeling* that the place gives you. You could say that this place has a creepy atmosphere.'

There was silence. He opened his eyes. Izzy and Max had disappeared. Ralph suddenly felt very cold and alone.

What a feeling

Read the opening sentences of the stories below. Which word from the list on the right best describes the atmosphere? Link each sentence with the correct atmosphere word.

1 The door slowly creaked open but no one was there.

2 The sun shone brightly and the children played.

3 The wind howled through the trees, the shadows grew and darkness fell.

4 Gripping the bar grimly, our knuckles were white as the roller coaster slowly approached the summit.

5 The study door was still locked and there seemed no way anyone could have entered, but the money had gone.

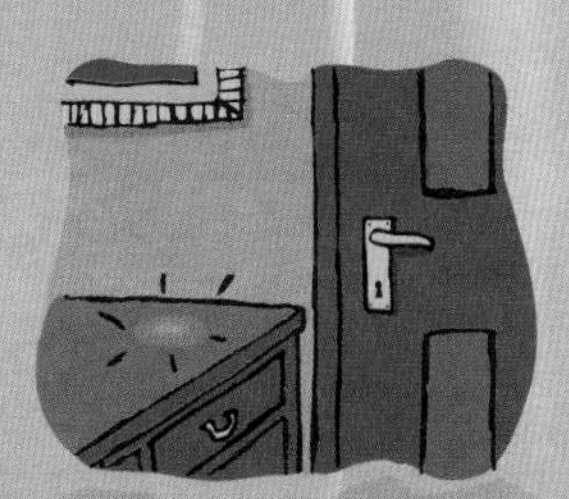

MYSTERIOUS

CREEPY

HAPPY

TENSE

FRIGHTENING

TOP TIP

You can create a sense of atmosphere through description. Note down the powerful nouns, verbs and adjectives that are used by the writers you enjoy.

DID YOU KNOW?

The word atmosphere is also the name given to the gases surrounding the Earth. It comes from the Greek words *atmos* meaning 'vapour' and *sphaira* meaning 'globe'.

Vivid or what?

Izzy had to write a ghost story for her descriptive writing homework. To get some inspiration, she decided to visit the manor house again.

She knew that adjectives and adverbs were important when writing effective description, so she started jotting down a few adjectives as she walked from room to room.

GREY

HISTORIC

OLD-FASHIONED

SOLEMN

THREADBARE

She looked down at what she had written. The first letter of each word was glowing slightly in the gathering gloom. A shiver went down her spine – these letters spelt GHOST!

Izzy decided that she was now quite inspired enough. It was definitely time to head home – fast!

Transformations

Match up the verbs below with the endings on the right. The result in each case will be an adjective, e.g. 'hurt' + 'ful' = 'hurtful'. Note that sometimes you have to change the form of the verb, e.g. 'defend' + '-sive' = 'defensive'.

love	-some
please	-ic
explode	-able
quarrel	-ant
sympathise	-ful
hope	-sive

Now do the same, but this time turning nouns into adjectives.

fool	-ic
child	-ly
sand	-al
hero	-ish
music	-y
friend	-like

• TOP TIPS •

Adjectives are words that give information about nouns:

- **the *heavy* parcel**
- **a *four-wheeled* motorbike.**

Adverbs are words that tell you more about the verb, or about the sentence as a whole:

- **she laughed *hysterically***
- **they got here *yesterday*.**

DID YOU KNOW?

The adjective used to describe someone who spits a lot is 'sputative'. It comes from the Latin word *sputum* meaning saliva or mucus spat out. Another strange adjective is the word 'thaumaturgical', which means melting. It comes from the Old English word *thawian*, which means 'thaw'.

Test your knowledge 3

1 State three ways in which writers make the characters in their stories come alive.

a) ....

b) ....

c) ....

(6 marks)

2 a) What is DIALOGUE?

....

b) What kind of punctuation do you use when writing dialogue?

....

c) What kind of narration is 'He felt angry at the way he had been ignored'?

....

d) What kind of narration is 'I woke up this morning and felt very excited'?

....

(4 marks)

3 a) What is the SETTING of a story?

....

b) What is the ATMOSPHERE of a story?

....

(2 marks)

4 a) What is an adjective?

....

b) Read the following passage and underline the adjectives:

> The bright sunlight shines through the yellow curtains making the whole room shine with light. As she pulled back the curtains and saw the blue, cloudless sky, she knew it was going to be a wonderful day.

(8 marks)

5 Look at the following nouns and change them into adjectives, e.g. 'mountain' becomes 'mountainous'.

a) circle ....

b) trouble ....

c) giant ....

d) parent ....

(4 marks)

6 a) What is an adverb?

....

b) Read the following and underline the adverbs:

The teacher moved quickly over to the group in the corner who were laughing loudly. As he approached, one of the boys turned suddenly and grinned broadly at his friend.

c) Use the correct adverb from the list to complete each sentence:

(i) The starving man ate ....

(ii) The cat stretched ....

(iii) The alarm rang ....

(iv) The girl whispered ....

(v) The boy stuck his tongue out ....

lazily cheekily hungrily loudly quietly

(11 marks)

(Total 35 marks)

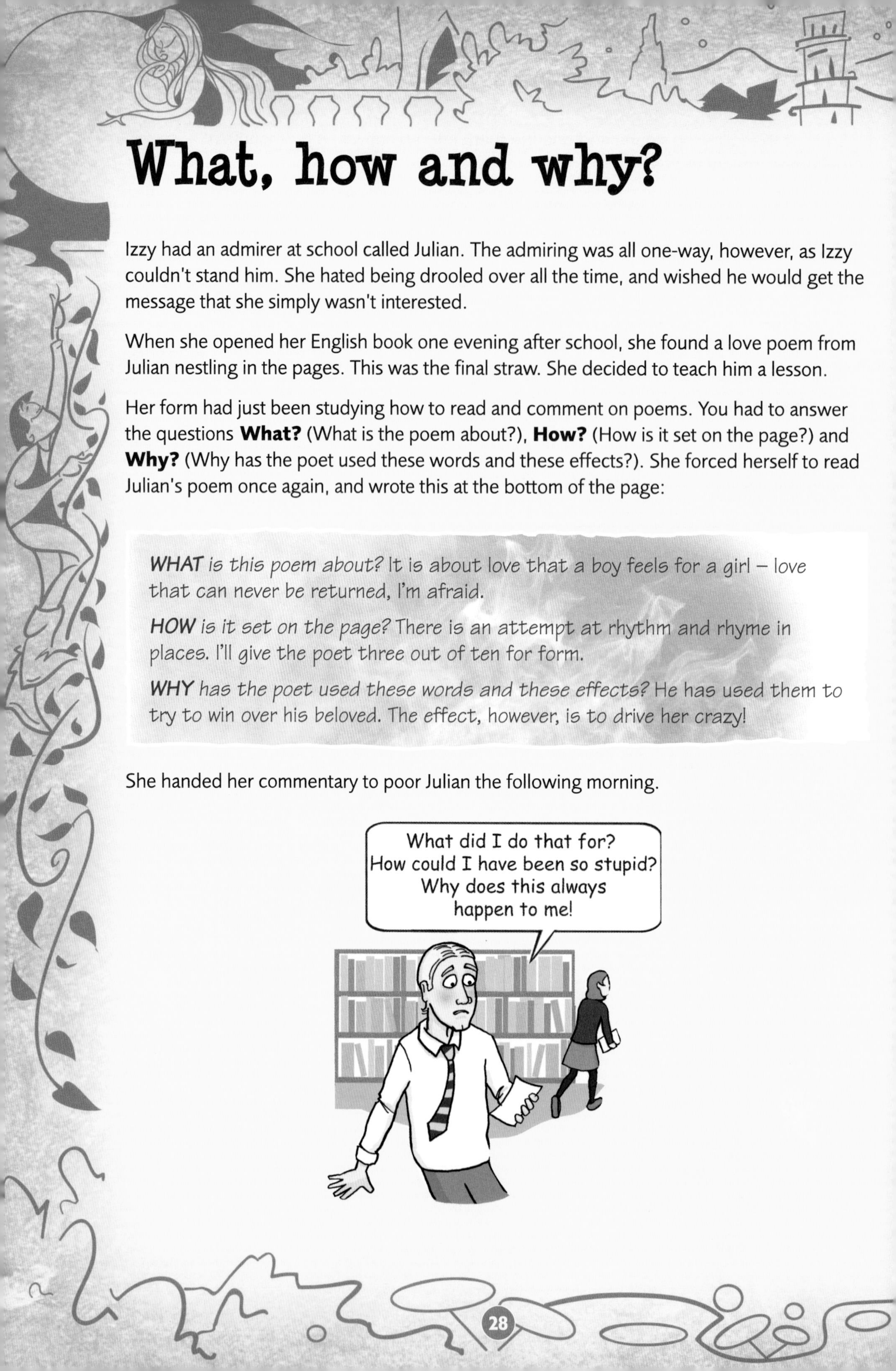

What, how and why?

Izzy had an admirer at school called Julian. The admiring was all one-way, however, as Izzy couldn't stand him. She hated being drooled over all the time, and wished he would get the message that she simply wasn't interested.

When she opened her English book one evening after school, she found a love poem from Julian nestling in the pages. This was the final straw. She decided to teach him a lesson.

Her form had just been studying how to read and comment on poems. You had to answer the questions **What?** (What is the poem about?), **How?** (How is it set on the page?) and **Why?** (Why has the poet used these words and these effects?). She forced herself to read Julian's poem once again, and wrote this at the bottom of the page:

WHAT is this poem about? It is about love that a boy feels for a girl – love that can never be returned, I'm afraid.

HOW is it set on the page? There is an attempt at rhythm and rhyme in places. I'll give the poet three out of ten for form.

WHY has the poet used these words and these effects? He has used them to try to win over his beloved. The effect, however, is to drive her crazy!

She handed her commentary to poor Julian the following morning.

All about poetry

Use the clues to find the missing words and complete the puzzle.

Across

4 It can help you to understand a poem if you read it out ....
5 The material the poet writes about is sometimes called the ....
6 When approaching a poem, your first step is to .... it carefully.
8 Tone in a poem is closely linked with the .... the poet creates.
10 The ideas the poet writes about is sometimes called the poem's ....
11 One popular modern poet is called Simon ....

Down

1 A narrative poem told through the eyes of one of the characters is told in the .... person.
2 Someone who writes poetry is called a ....
3 Poets choose their .... carefully when writing their poems.
5 Famous poem by Ted Hughes, named after a big black bird.
7 Poets use language in particular ways to create their ....
9 A famous First World War poet is called Wilfred ....

• TOP TIPS •

When reading a poem for the first time don't worry too much about understanding every detail. Try to get a general impression of what it is about – look for key points and questions it raises.

DID YOU KNOW?

Poetry is one of the oldest forms of writing in the world. Poetry was written by the ancient Greeks as long ago as 700 BC, but it is thought that poetry existed even long before that.

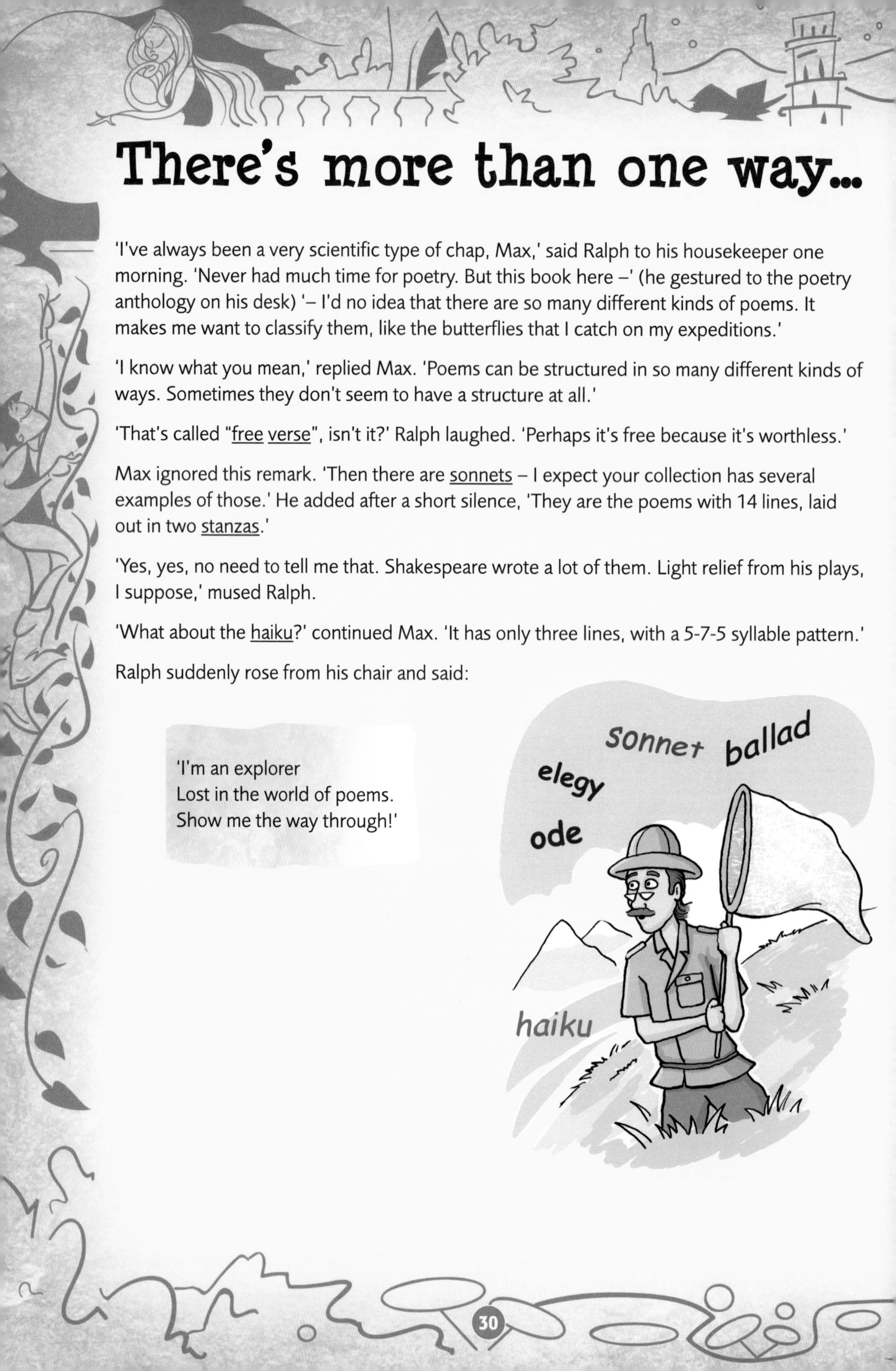

There's more than one way...

'I've always been a very scientific type of chap, Max,' said Ralph to his housekeeper one morning. 'Never had much time for poetry. But this book here –' (he gestured to the poetry anthology on his desk) '– I'd no idea that there are so many different kinds of poems. It makes me want to classify them, like the butterflies that I catch on my expeditions.'

'I know what you mean,' replied Max. 'Poems can be structured in so many different kinds of ways. Sometimes they don't seem to have a structure at all.'

'That's called "free verse", isn't it?' Ralph laughed. 'Perhaps it's free because it's worthless.'

Max ignored this remark. 'Then there are sonnets – I expect your collection has several examples of those.' He added after a short silence, 'They are the poems with 14 lines, laid out in two stanzas.'

'Yes, yes, no need to tell me that. Shakespeare wrote a lot of them. Light relief from his plays, I suppose,' mused Ralph.

'What about the haiku?' continued Max. 'It has only three lines, with a 5-7-5 syllable pattern.'

Ralph suddenly rose from his chair and said:

'I'm an explorer
Lost in the world of poems.
Show me the way through!'

Types of poem

All the following describe types of poems or verse, or are to do with the different structures that poems can have. See if you can unscramble the anagrams to find the answers.

1	A poem with 14 lines	NETNSO
2	A humorous poem with five lines	IREMKICL
3	A long song or poem that tells a story	DALABL
4	A Japanese verse form	UIKAH
5	Verse that has no rhyme or regular rhythm	REEF SEVER
6	A verse in a poem	ZNSTAA
7	A poem written in praise of someone or something	DEO
8	The name for the regular beat in a poem	THMYRH
9	A sad poem or song	EYEGL
10	The basic unit of a poem	NILE

DID YOU KNOW?

In 2002 the writer Valerie Laws spray-painted words from a poem onto a flock of sheep. She wanted to see if the animals would arrange themselves to make a new poem as they wandered around the field – and they did!

• TOP TIPS •

The key to understanding how a poem works is to look at how the poet has structured it. Ask yourself these questions:

- **Has the poet used stanzas?**
- **Is there a pattern of rhythm?**
- **Is rhyme used?**
- **Are the lines of a regular length?**

The main thing you should ask yourself when identifying any of these features is, 'What effect do they have on the poem?'

I've got rhythm, I've got rhyme

Izzy sat down and looked carefully at the poem she had been given for homework.

'Now,' thought Izzy to herself, 'let's have a look at this.' She consulted the notes she had made in her notebook during the lesson.

'Rhyme and rhythm – that's what I need to look for.' She looked again at the poem. 'Hmm, *Night Mail* by WH Auden. I'll try reading it aloud – that might help me feel the rhythm.' Izzy read out the first few lines –

> 'This is the Night Mail crossing the Border,
> Bringing the cheque and the postal order,
>
> Letters from the rich, letters from the poor,
> The shop at the corner, the girl next door.'

She then read the lines again, tapping out the rhythm with her pencil on the desk.

'*Tappity tap tap, tappity tap tap*. That sounds like the rhythm of the train's wheels going over the tracks,' she thought. 'What about the rhyme. Yes, there's rhyme too. The lines rhyme together in pairs. I remember our teacher telling us that when that happened they were called rhyming couplets. The rhyme helps to emphasise the sound too.'

Izzy wrote down her ideas on the rhyme and rhythm of the poem.

'Good. Now that's done I think I'll have some rhythm of a different kind,' she said to herself, reaching for her MP3 player.

Making it rhyme

The following two stanzas are from a poem called 'The Daffodils' by William Wordsworth.

The poem rhymes but the final words have all been put in a box and jumbled up. Add the correct words to the end of each line to make the poem rhyme (and make sense!).

Hint: the rhyme scheme is ABABCC.

I wandered lonely as a ....
That floats on high o'er vales and ....
When all at once I saw a ....
A host of golden ....
Beside the lake, beneath the ....
Fluttering and dancing in the ....

Continuous as the stars that ....
And twinkle on the milky ....
They stretched in never-ending ....
Along the margin of a ....
Then thousand saw I at a ....
Tossing their heads in sprightly ....

crowd
dance
way
hills
daffodils
line
shine
glance
cloud
bay
breeze
trees

DID YOU KNOW?

Ring a ring o' roses,
A pocket full of posies,
A – tishoo! A – tishoo!
We all fall down.

This nursery rhyme originates from the time of the Great Plague (1665). The 'roses' are the rosy coloured circular rashes that developed on someone who had caught the plague, and the 'posies' were the little bundles of herbs said to ward off the plague. Sneezing was a symptom of the plague – before the person who had caught it 'fell down' dead.

TOP TIP

Don't just spot rhyme and rhythm in poems – think about what effects they create on the ear and in the mind.

Test your knowledge 4

1 a) What is RHYME in a poem?

....

b) What is RHYTHM in a poem?

....

c) Do all poems rhyme?

....

(6 marks)

2 a) How many lines does a sonnet have?

....

b) What is a stanza?

....

(4 marks)

3 What kind of poem is this?

The wind blew all night
And on, on through the next day
It had no ending.

....

(3 marks)

4 What kind of poem tells a story?

....

(2 marks)

5 What kind of poem was originally sung?

....

(2 marks)

6 What kind of poem is this?

There was an old man who, when little,
Fell casually into a kettle,
But growing too stout
He could never get out –
So he passed all his life in that kettle.

....

(3 marks)

7 How many syllables are there in each of these lines?

a) She walks in beauty, like the night ....

b) Of cloudless climes and starry skies ....

c) Gather ye rosebuds while ye may ....

d) See the kitten on the wall ....

e) Sporting with leaves that fall ....

(15 marks)

(Total 35 marks)

Picture this!

Izzy had downloaded some photographs onto her computer from her digital camera. She noticed how her computer program labelled them as Image 1, Image 2, Image 3 and so on.

'That's where the word "imagery" comes from, I suppose,' she thought out loud. 'Imagery means pictures. The poem I was reading earlier also had images in it, but those images weren't created by pictures – they were created in my mind by the words that the poet used.'

She thought back to her English lesson earlier that day. They had been reading part of a poem called 'The Ancient Mariner', which told the story of a sailor who had shot an albatross and brought bad luck on all his ship mates. Some of the imagery had made a vivid impression in her mind:

> 'The ship drove fast, loud roared the blast,
> And southward aye we fled.
> And now there came both mist and snow,
> And it grew wondrous cold:
> And ice, mast-high, came floating by,
> As green as emerald.'

'That imagery was so vivid I could almost feel the cold.' She shivered as she thought about it.

Search for the image words

Several things that help to create images in poems are hidden in the wordsearch. Can you find them all?

X	O	N	O	M	A	T	O	P	O	E	I	A	P
N	A	C	R	H	D	M	V	M	M	R	E	D	E
O	T	M	S	O	J	V	T	B	K	T	U	V	R
I	T	A	S	T	E	K	L	P	J	E	W	E	S
T	O	A	W	B	C	D	M	C	Y	R	N	R	O
A	U	Z	F	L	T	L	M	V	V	U	R	B	N
R	C	E	E	N	I	P	E	H	G	O	L	S	I
E	H	O	U	O	V	C	E	N	S	L	A	N	F
T	R	A	T	M	E	T	A	P	H	O	R	S	I
I	A	S	N	R	S	I	G	H	T	C	D	M	C
L	C	E	E	H	E	O	L	D	S	T	E	E	A
L	Y	L	M	L	T	F	U	E	N	E	V	L	T
A	T	I	E	L	P	D	Q	N	W	B	N	L	I
S	N	M	V	T	H	C	A	R	D	W	S	D	O
I	S	I	O	E	U	P	D	X	E	S	A	R	N
O	A	S	M	N	O	I	T	O	M	E	S	A	N

adjectives
metaphors
onomatopoeia
smell
adverbs
personification
colour
sounds
similes
alliteration
taste
sight
emotion
touch
movement

DID YOU KNOW?

Imagery is often used in short stories and novels. The horror story writer Edgar Allan Poe was a master of imagery. In his story *The Murders in the Rue Morgue*, he used strong visual imagery to describe the scene where bodies were discovered –

'On a chair lay a razor, besmeared with blood. On the hearth were two or three long thick tresses of grey human hair, also dabbled in blood, and seeming to have been pulled up by the roots.'

Some of his imagery was so powerful that people complained about it.

• TOP TIPS •

There are many things that can be used to create images in the mind of the reader, for example:

- **vivid description**
- **metaphors**
- **similes**
- **sound effects**
- **the use of words or descriptions that appeal to the senses, e.g. the sweet and tangy orange.**

Crash!

Izzy and her dad were taking Spotless for a walk in the park.

'We've been learning about sound effects in writing in English this week, Dad,' said Izzy.

'What have you learnt?' asked Ralph.

'Well, there's assonance for a start – that's where vowel sounds are repeated, like "On hearing the tale he went pale fearing the worst." And then there's alliteration, which is the repetition of the same sound at the beginning of the words.' Izzy started spouting a string of alliterative phrases to illustrate her point –

'I slid slowly down the slippery path. The rabbit ran round and round the rocky hill. The snake slithered silently...'

A huge crash cut her off in mid-flow and made them both jump. A boy's shot at goal had gone a little off course and the football had smashed through the roof of a nearby greenhouse.

'Yelp! Woof, woof, woof!' The crash had made Spotless jump too and he was now cowering behind Ralph's legs, shaking.

'Lots of examples of the third kind of sound effect there,' said Izzy, recovering her composure. 'Crash, yelp and woof.'

'Don't tell me,' said Ralph, 'onomatopoeia.'

'That's right,' said Izzy. 'Got it in one.'

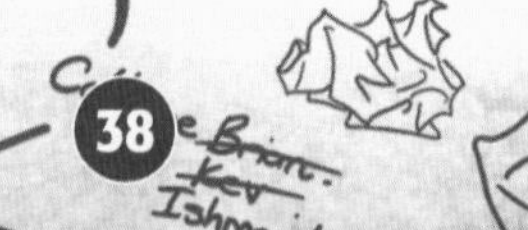

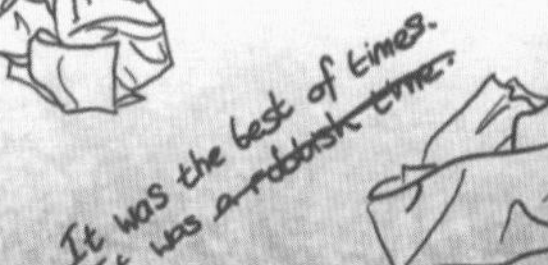

Use the right term

Link these phrases to the right word.

1 The slithery snake slid through the grass.

2 The baker decided to throw away the mouldy dough.

3 The plates fell over with a crash.

4 The teacher told the class to hush.

5 The rampaging robot ran out of control.

6 The door blew shut with a bang.

7 The gift was bought with thought.

8 The memory of the place and that face began to fade.

alliteration

assonance

onomatopoeia

DID YOU KNOW?

The collective technical name for words that create sound effects is phonological features. The word comes from the Greek *phone*, which means 'sound'. This is a common prefix and suffix in many English words, such as 'telephone' and 'saxophone'.

• TOP TIP •

Make sure you can:

- **identify each feature**
- **use its proper technical name**
- **describe the effect it has on the poem.**

For example: 'The phrase "the slithery snake" is an example of alliteration. It emphasises the hissing noise that the snake makes, as well as the shape of the snake's body through the shape of the initial letter S.'

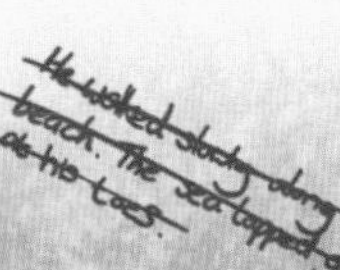

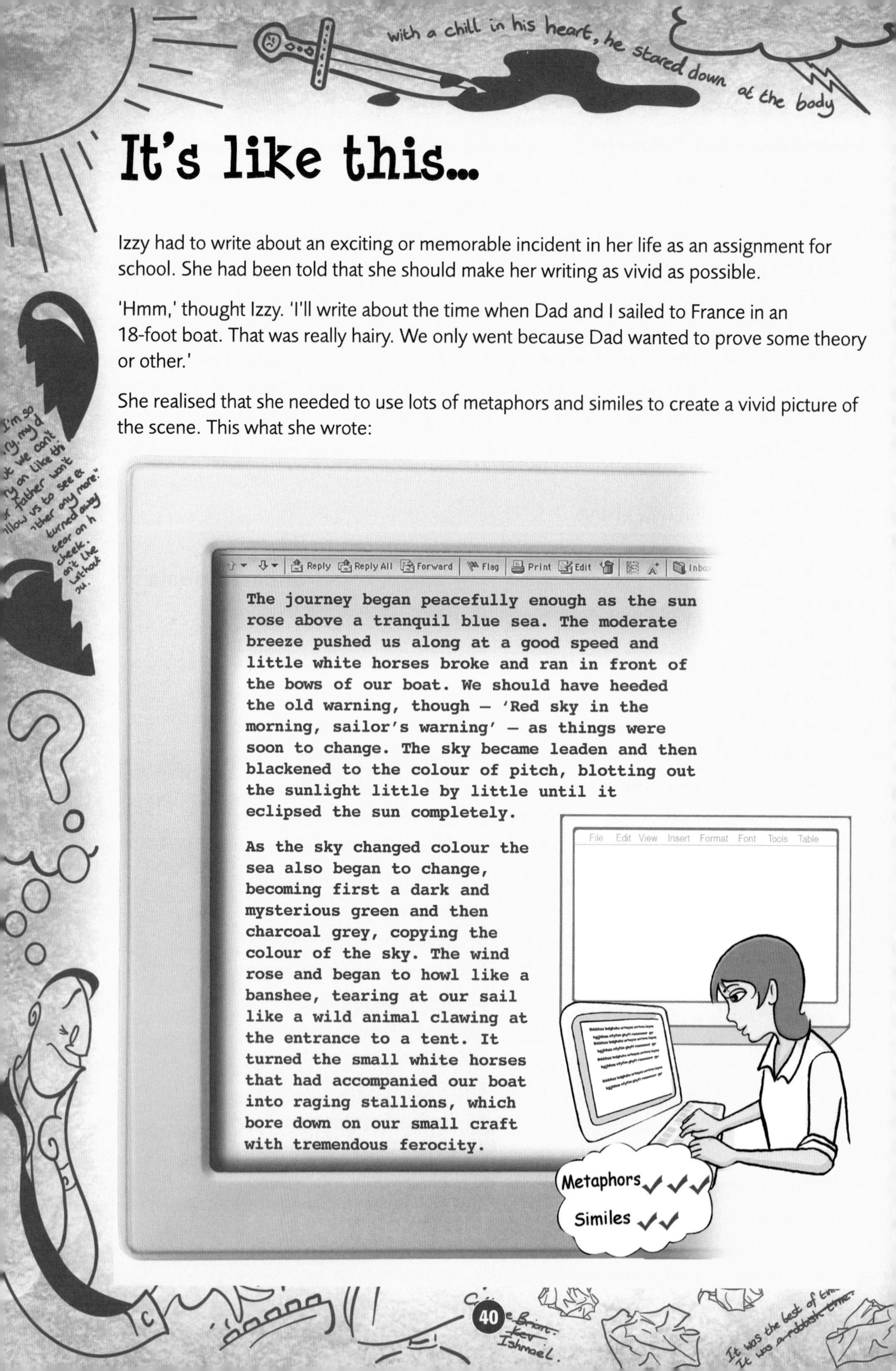

It's like this...

Izzy had to write about an exciting or memorable incident in her life as an assignment for school. She had been told that she should make her writing as vivid as possible.

'Hmm,' thought Izzy. 'I'll write about the time when Dad and I sailed to France in an 18-foot boat. That was really hairy. We only went because Dad wanted to prove some theory or other.'

She realised that she needed to use lots of metaphors and similes to create a vivid picture of the scene. This what she wrote:

The journey began peacefully enough as the sun rose above a tranquil blue sea. The moderate breeze pushed us along at a good speed and little white horses broke and ran in front of the bows of our boat. We should have heeded the old warning, though – 'Red sky in the morning, sailor's warning' – as things were soon to change. The sky became leaden and then blackened to the colour of pitch, blotting out the sunlight little by little until it eclipsed the sun completely.

As the sky changed colour the sea also began to change, becoming first a dark and mysterious green and then charcoal grey, copying the colour of the sky. The wind rose and began to howl like a banshee, tearing at our sail like a wild animal clawing at the entrance to a tent. It turned the small white horses that had accompanied our boat into raging stallions, which bore down on our small craft with tremendous ferocity.

Word snake

Work your way along the snake by finding the word that completes the simile or metaphor in each case.

1 As black as ....

2 It is like holding back the ....

3 It sounds like there is an .... in here.

4 The jacket was the colour of an ....

5 As dull as ....

6 Her laugh was like the neigh of a ....

7 As slippery as an ....

8 She is a shining .... in the community.

9 He was a .... of strength.

10 She went as .... as a beetroot.

11 This is as dry as ....

12 He is as tall as a ....

• TOP TIPS •

Remember:

- **A simile compares two things by using such words as 'like' or 'as', e.g. 'George ate like a pig.'**
- **A metaphor compares two things more directly, without using 'like' or 'as', e.g. 'The news was a bolt from the blue.'**

Start

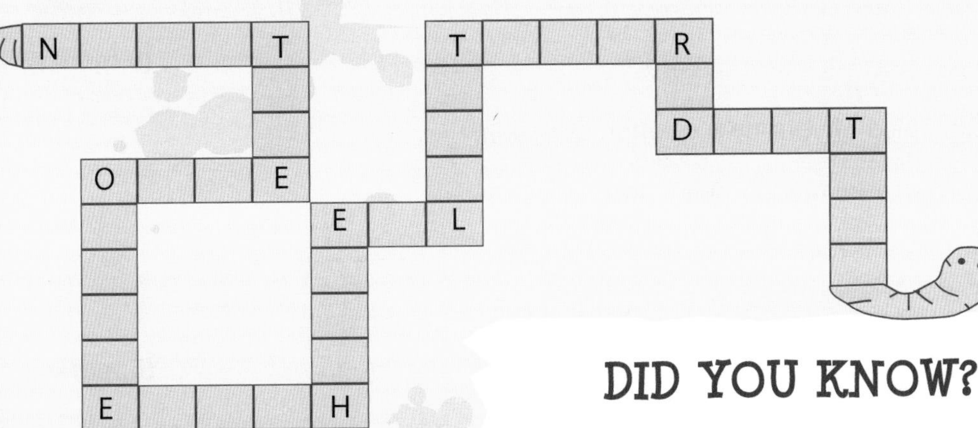

DID YOU KNOW?

A 'dead metaphor' is one that has been used so much over the years that it has become a part of everyday language, e.g. 'tying up loose ends'. A 'mixed metaphor' is one that mixes up two separate ideas and can often sound very silly, e.g. 'her words struck a chord that pierced me to the heart'.

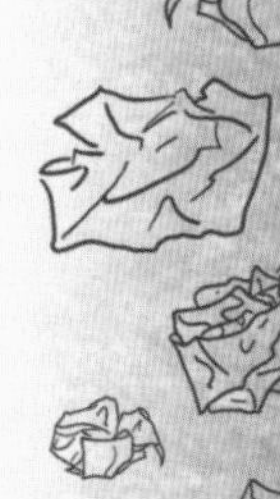

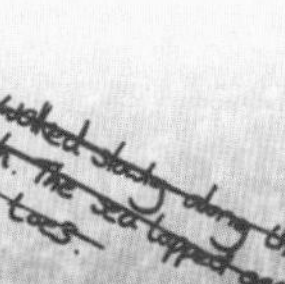

Test your knowledge 5

1 What is a simile? ……………………………………………………………………………

(2 marks)

2 What is a metaphor? ……………………………………………………………………………

(2 marks)

3 Complete these well-known similes:

a) as dry as a ……………………………………………………………………………

b) as heavy as ……………………………………………………………………………

c) as light as a ……………………………………………………………………………

d) as clean as a ……………………………………………………………………………

e) as white as a ……………………………………………………………………………

f) as sly as a ……………………………………………………………………………

(6 marks)

4 What is onomatopoeia?

……………………………………………………………………………

(3 marks)

5 Write three examples of your own of onomatopoeia.

a) ……………………………………………………………………………

b) ……………………………………………………………………………

c) ……………………………………………………………………………

(6 marks)

6 What poetic technique is each of these lines an example of?

a) 'The wind stood up and gave a shout.'

....

b) 'Dirty British coaster with a salt-caked smoke stack
Butting through the channel in the mad March days.'

....

c) 'The moon was a ghostly galleon tossed upon cloudy seas'

....

d) 'Lightning cracked like explosions in the sky.'

....

(8 marks)

7 Read the following two stanzas and identify the underlined features:

> Over the cobbles he clattered and clashed in the dark inn-yard,
> And he tapped with his whip on the shutters, but all was locked and barred:
> He whistled a tune to the window; and who should be waiting there
> But the landlord's black-eyed daughter,
>   Bess, the landlord's daughter,
> Plaiting a dark red love-knot into her long black hair.

> And in the dark old inn-yard a stable-wicket creaked
> Where Tim, the ostler, listened; his face was white and peaked,
> His eyes were hollows of madness, his hair like mouldy hay;
> But he loved the landlord's daughter,
>   The landlord's red-lipped daughter:
> Dumb as a dog he listened, and he heard the robber say –

(8 marks)

(Total 35 marks)

It's all an act

'Max has been behaving in a most extraordinary way recently,' thought Izzy. She would catch him talking to himself for minutes on end, and adopting the most dramatic poses, only to snap out of it suddenly when he realised he was being overheard. He also kept having long discussions on the phone with his friend, Beth.

Whenever Izzy asked Max what this was all about, he pretended that there was nothing going on. But a twinkle in his eye showed her that something was afoot.

'Have you seen that Macbeth is on at the Village Hall next week, Max?' asked Izzy.

'Is it really?' replied Max.

'Yes, we're studying that in school soon so Dad and I are going to see it. It's one of Shakespeare's greatest tragedies. I don't know much about it but it's bound to end with the death of some of the characters. All the tragedies do. Not like the comedies, which have happy endings.

'What else do you know about Shakespeare's plays?' asked Max.

'Well, they're written mainly in blank verse, which is verse that doesn't rhyme. They also contain lots of long speeches and soliloquies, where a character is alone on the stage when they're speaking.'

'Yes,' replied Max. 'Shakespeare uses all kinds of **dramatic techniques**.'

The following week Izzy and Ralph were sitting in the front row of the packed village hall waiting for Macbeth to start. They were entranced from the opening scene, when three witches cackled together over a cauldron, their voices battling against thunder and rain bellowing from the wings.

As soon as Macbeth himself strode onto the stage, they nearly fell off their chairs in surprise – it was Max! So that was what he had been doing all these past weeks – practising his lines! He had obviously done an excellent job of it, because the performance was gripping. His friend Beth was playing opposite him as Lady Macbeth. 'Very suitable,' thought Ralph, 'as she was always a bit of a schemer.'

Criss cross

Fill in the words to complete the criss cross. One word has been given to start you off.

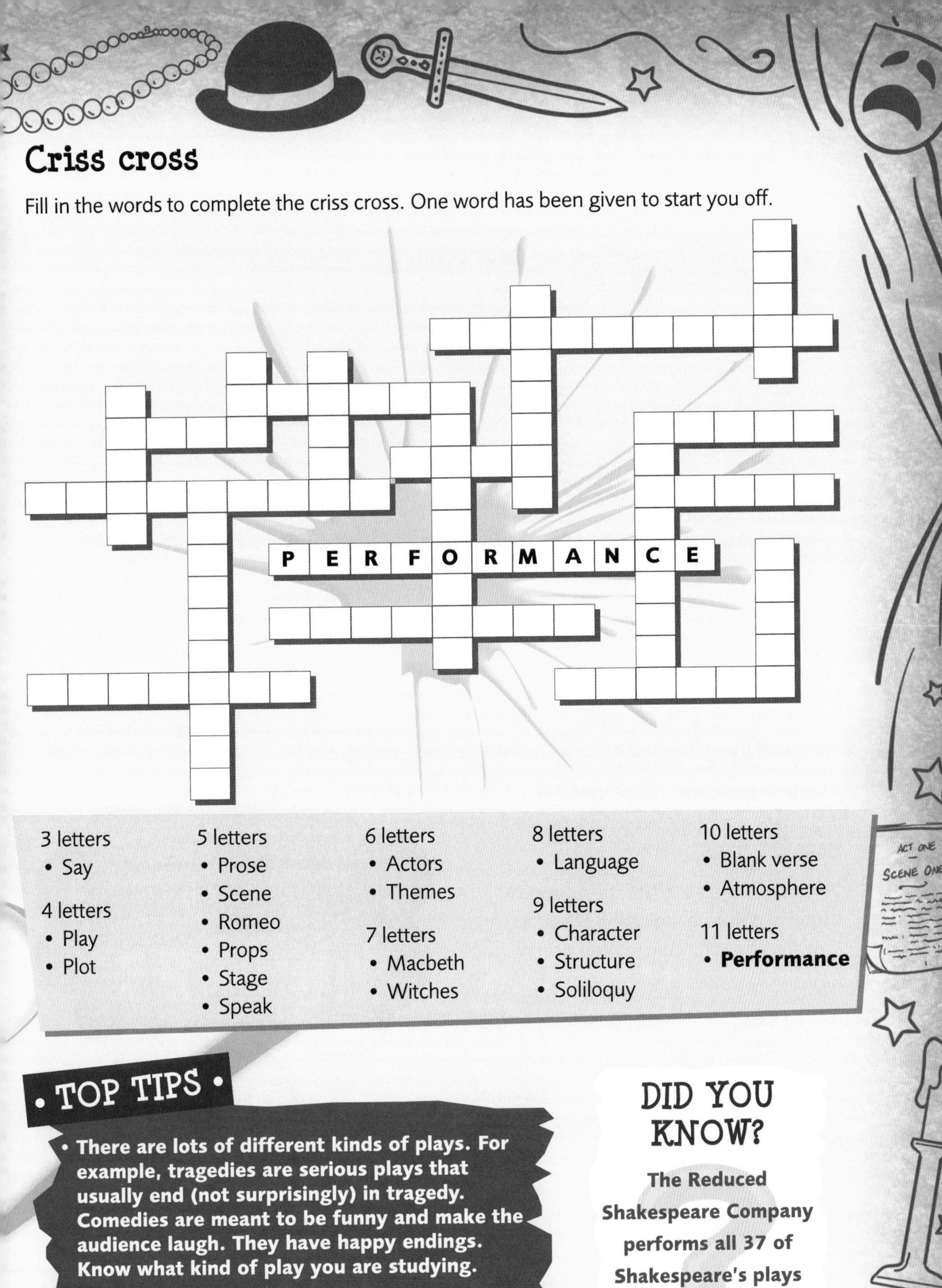

3 letters	5 letters	6 letters	8 letters	10 letters
• Say	• Prose	• Actors	• Language	• Blank verse
	• Scene	• Themes		• Atmosphere
4 letters	• Romeo	**7 letters**	**9 letters**	**11 letters**
• Play	• Props	• Macbeth	• Character	• **Performance**
• Plot	• Stage	• Witches	• Structure	
	• Speak		• Soliloquy	

• TOP TIPS •

- **There are lots of different kinds of plays. For example, tragedies are serious plays that usually end (not surprisingly) in tragedy. Comedies are meant to be funny and make the audience laugh. They have happy endings. Know what kind of play you are studying.**
- **When you read a play, remember that it was written to be performed rather than read.**

DID YOU KNOW?

The Reduced Shakespeare Company performs all 37 of Shakespeare's plays and 154 sonnets in just 90 minutes.

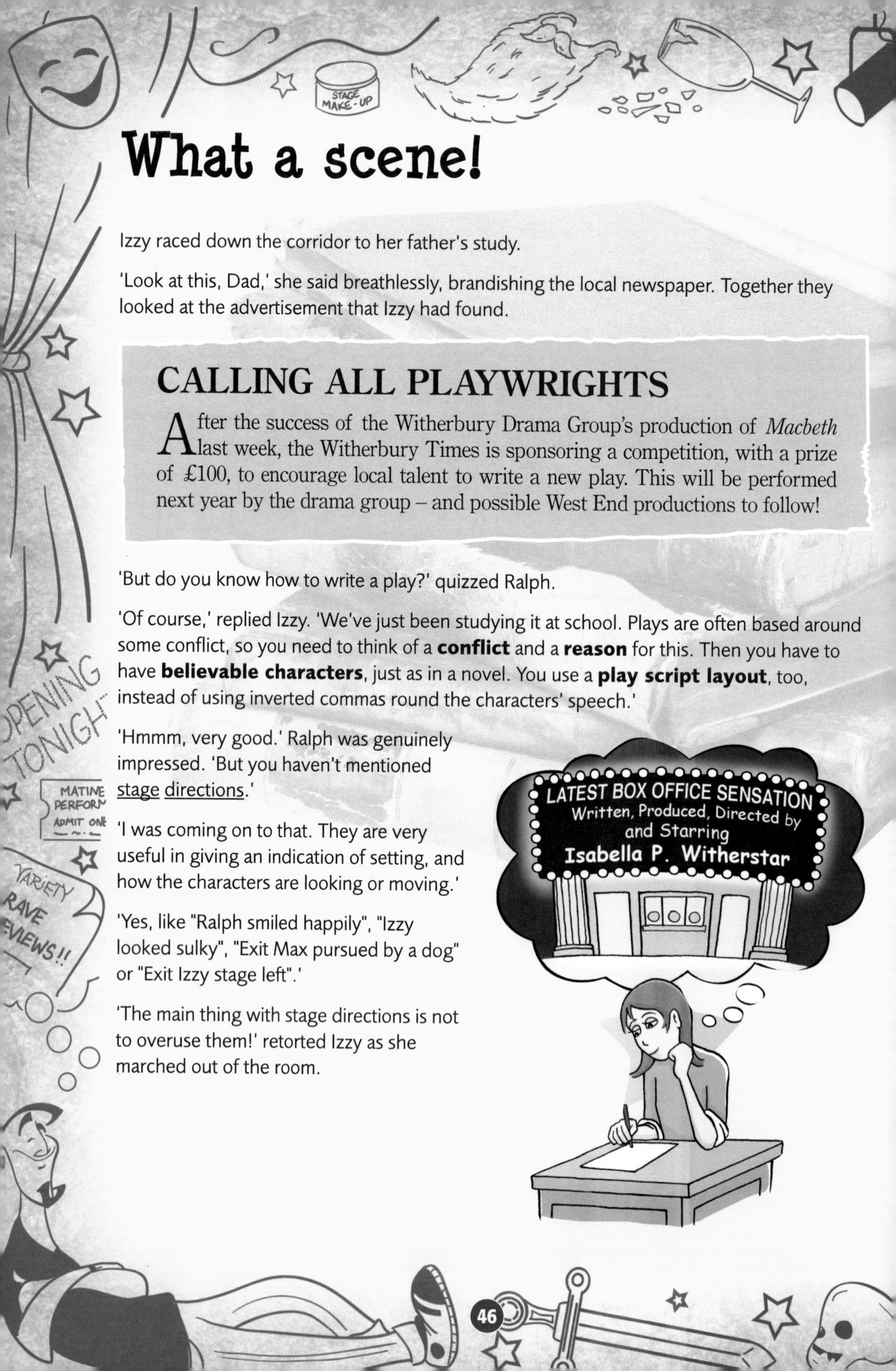

What a scene!

Izzy raced down the corridor to her father's study.

'Look at this, Dad,' she said breathlessly, brandishing the local newspaper. Together they looked at the advertisement that Izzy had found.

CALLING ALL PLAYWRIGHTS

After the success of the Witherbury Drama Group's production of *Macbeth* last week, the Witherbury Times is sponsoring a competition, with a prize of £100, to encourage local talent to write a new play. This will be performed next year by the drama group – and possible West End productions to follow!

'But do you know how to write a play?' quizzed Ralph.

'Of course,' replied Izzy. 'We've just been studying it at school. Plays are often based around some conflict, so you need to think of a **conflict** and a **reason** for this. Then you have to have **believable characters**, just as in a novel. You use a **play script layout**, too, instead of using inverted commas round the characters' speech.'

'Hmmm, very good.' Ralph was genuinely impressed. 'But you haven't mentioned stage directions.'

'I was coming on to that. They are very useful in giving an indication of setting, and how the characters are looking or moving.'

'Yes, like "Ralph smiled happily", "Izzy looked sulky", "Exit Max pursued by a dog" or "Exit Izzy stage left".'

'The main thing with stage directions is not to overuse them!' retorted Izzy as she marched out of the room.

Playscript puzzle

Use the clues to find the missing words.

1 When writing your play you should make sure your .... captures the audience's attention.

2 The term for the storyline of a play.

3 You might want to put in .... directions to help the actors know how to move, look etc.

4 Think carefully about what your characters ....

5 You might want the characters to give longer ....

6 Your play should contain convincing ....

7 You will need to decide if your actors will use ...., such as swords, drinking mugs etc.

8 The high point of your play is called the ....

9 You should not use .... when writing out your playscript.

10 To keep your audience gripped by your play you need to create ....

• TOP TIPS •

When writing a play:

- **think up a good plot**
- **make sure your characters are convincing**
- **plan your play carefully**
- **use stage directions if you need them**
- **open and close your play effectively**
- **don't use speech marks.**

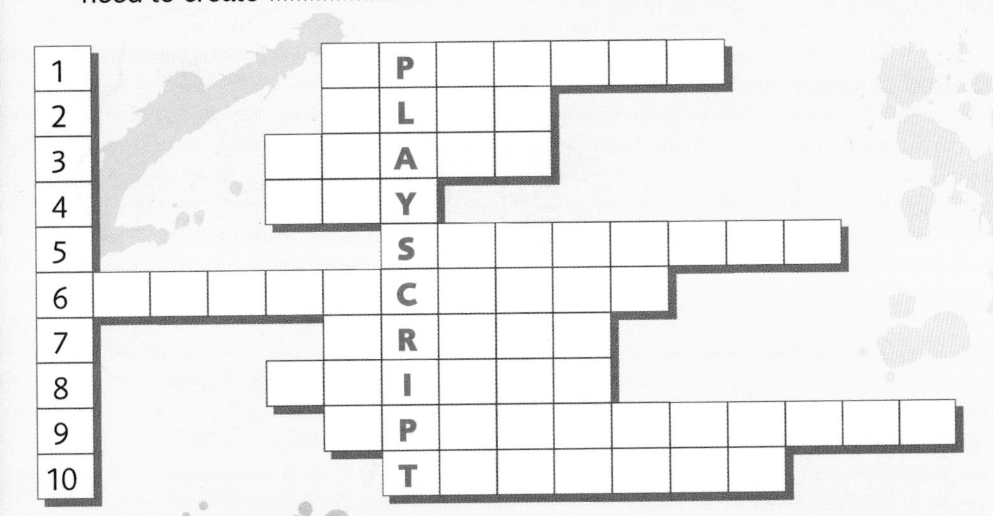

DID YOU KNOW?

Samuel Beckett's play *Breath*, which was first performed in 1970, lasts only 30 seconds and has no characters and no dialogue.

What a life

Ralph's failure to engage a suitable writer to help with his autobiography did not deter him.

'I'll just have to do it all myself,' he told Max grimly. 'After all, when my crew all abandoned me on my attempt to sail round the world dressed in armour, I didn't give up, did I?'

'So perhaps I should begin with that very story,' Ralph continued. 'Let me see...

"Ralph, the heroic adventurer, looked out across the ocean through the narrow gap in his visor. His crew were by now a mere speck in the distance and very soon they had disappeared altogether. Ralph was completely alone in the midst of a vast and hostile ocean. At first all went well. The sea was calm and the armour did not seem to be too heavy. However, very soon all was to change – and not for the better. That evening, as the sun went down, black, ominous storm clouds began to gather on the horizon. The tranquil sea darkened and Ralph's boat began to wallow as waves began to form and grow bigger."'

A cough from his butler stopped him in his tracks. 'May I point out, Sir, that autobiographies are written in the first person? And don't forget that they are generally organised chronologically, that is –'

'I know very well what that means, thank you,' retorted Ralph. 'But it's also very effective to begin with a dramatic moment in one's life, then deal with all the birth and childhood stuff in chapter two.'

He paused for a moment. 'I just wish I could remember anything in my life before the age of 36, that's all,' he added with a sigh.

Autobiography tips

The paragraph below gives you tips on how to write your own autobiography. Some of the words are scrambled. Can you unscramble them?

When you write an autobiography, you should use **trifs senrop ratrianon**.

Narrate the events of your life in **honricogollac rerod**.

Group the events in a logical way, and write a **hercapt** on each.

Before you start, you should have **delnanp ti racfelyul**, of course, and made lots of **tones**.

DID YOU KNOW?

The Diary of Anne Frank **is the world's best-selling diary. In this diary, Anne tells us what happened to her and her family when they went into hiding in Amsterdam to escape the Nazis during the Second World War. It has been translated into 55 languages and has sold more than 25 million copies world wide.**

• TOP TIPS •

When writing your autobiography:

- **plan your ideas carefully**
- **include interesting events and episodes**
- **make sure you write in the first person.**

Test your knowledge 6

1 Why is the opening of a play important?

....

(1 mark)

2 What kind of play is a tragedy?

....

(1 mark)

3 What kind of play is a comedy?

....

(1 mark)

4 Name two plays written by William Shakespeare.

a) ....

b) ....

(2 marks)

5 A famous Shakespearean theatre, now recreated on the banks of the River Thames in London, is called the ....

(1 mark)

6 Explain the following terms:

a) soliloquy ....

b) character ....

c) stage directions ....

d) scene ....

e) aside ....

f) props ....

g) dialogue ....

h) structure ....

i) themes ....

j) performance ....

k) role ....

l) setting ....

(12 marks)

7 Do you use speech marks when writing a play? ....

(1 mark)

8 Look at these two extracts from *Macbeth*. One is written in verse, and one in prose. Which is which, and can you explain your answer?

a)

> MACBETH
> Hang out our banners on the outward walls;
> The cry is still, 'They come !' Our castle's strength
> Will laugh a siege to scorn: here let them lie,
> Till famine and the ague eat them up.

b)

> PORTER
> Here's a knocking indeed! If a man were porter of hell-gate, he should have the turning of the key. (*Knocking)* Knock, knock, knock. Who's there in the name of Beelzebub?

....

....

....

(6 marks)

9 What is the difference between a biography and an autobiography?

....

(2 marks)

10 Complete these sentences:

a) A biography is written in the .... person.

b) An autobiography is written in the .... person.

(4 marks)

11 Another way that you can write about yourself and your own thoughts is by keeping a

....

(2 marks)

12 Why is The Diary of Anne Frank so famous?

....

....

(2 marks)

(Total 35 marks)

My Trip to Asia
by Stephen Cartwright

first arrived in India I was overwhelmed
intense heat. My guide took me to my w
otel, a magnificent 18th century marble

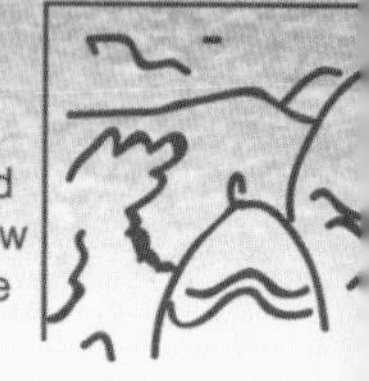

Did you see that film?

Izzy returned from the cinema one evening in a bad mood.

'Didn't you enjoy the film, Izzy?' asked Max.

'It was terrible, Max. It wasn't what I expected at all.'

'Why was that then?' asked Max.

'Well I'd read a review of it in *Film and TV* magazine the other day, which made it sound fantastic,' said Izzy. 'I don't agree with the reviewer's ideas at all.'

'I suppose reviewers are only putting forward their **opinion** of the film – or book, or CD, or whatever it is that is being reviewed. I must admit, they usually **support their view** by some sort of **analysis** or **evidence**, but it does come down to the reviewer's opinion in the end.'

'Well in *my* opinion it is a dreadful film,' Izzy continued. 'I'm going to write to the magazine and tell them.'

'Don't forget to back up your opinion with evidence and analysis!' said Max.

I have rarely seen a film in which the acting was so wooden and unconvincing, although it is hard to imagine the world's greatest actors being able to make anything interesting or exciting out of such a feeble script. These actors were far from the world's greatest though and the result is a completely missable film. Even the South American setting seemed to lack colour and vitality. In fact, I was left wondering why they had gone to the expense of filming in Rio. For all the good it did, they might as well have filmed it in Slough and saved themselves the money. Save your money too and give it a miss.

an astonishing blockbuster action movie with incredible special effects. From the mind-blowing title sequence to the end credits, the viewer is left gasping for air as Oscar-wiiner Arnold Stallone single-handedly takes on every bad guy in the whole world in a blistering 24 hours

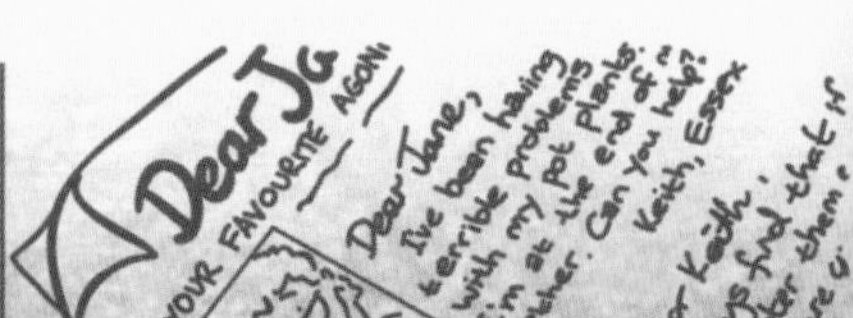

2 red onions, chopped
3 sun-dried tomatoes, chopped
500g lean minced beef
alt and ground black pepper

to the meat. Cover a
simmer briskly for 5
and cook, stirring oc
until the aubergine i
and it has absorbed

Which review?

Here are some extracts from reviews of various kinds. Read them and write underneath each one what is being reviewed. (Choose an item from the box on the right.)

1 The camerawork was stunning and the big screen made the most of the spectacular settings. Unfortunately the acting did not quite come up to that standard. Although there were outstanding performances from some supporting actors, the main roles seemed wooden and lacking in life.

....

2 This is much more than another 'shoot-em-up' – there's a real storyline to the action and the characters really seem to come to life. The difficulty levels are such that you'll really get value for money too. You'll have to work hard to get to level six on this one!

....

3 You'll find this a real page turner, which will keep you guessing right up to the final chapter. To say more would be to give too much away. Read it for yourself – but make sure that you have plenty of time, as you'll not want to put it down.

....

3 The sound quality of this album is outstanding. It's amazing what digital remastering can achieve. The tracks sound as if they were recorded yesterday. If you're a fan, you'll want this one in your collection.

....

5 The scene changes went smoothly and the designer had made full use of the stage. Lighting was spot on and added much to the atmosphere of the whole experience.

....

CD

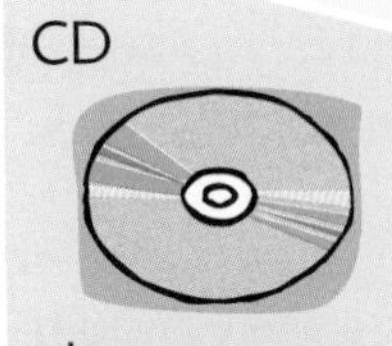

play

film

computer game

novel

• TOP TIPS •

When writing a review, make sure that you:

- **give your views on whatever it is that you are reviewing, but support them with evidence**
- **don't just retell the story of the film (or book, or play etc.) – pick out significant bits to give more detailed comment and to highlight the points you are making.**

DID YOU KNOW?

The author John Creasey received 774 rejection slips from publishers before getting his first book accepted. That first book was published in 1930 and received excellent reviews. Twenty-nine of his books were published in 1937, and in the end he had 562 published, making him one of the most prolific English writers.

Dear Editor,

I was appalled to re... in your column abou... the terrible rise in this country of incidents o... antisocial behaviour at village fetes. I mysel...

My Trip to Asia
by Stephen Cartwright

first arrived in India I was overwhelmed
intense heat. My guide took me to my w
otel, a magnificent 18th century marble

Every home should have one

'Have you seen this advertisement?' asked Max one day. The housekeeper put the magazine on Ralph's desk, covering up the plans of his latest invention.

'A remote controlled vacuum cleaner?' read Ralph. 'Hrrrrmph – I tried it myself a few years ago. Never quite worked, though...'

'Ah, yes. I remember we had to order quite a lot of new furniture after it ran wild when we were all out,' said Max. 'But this one looks fantastic.'

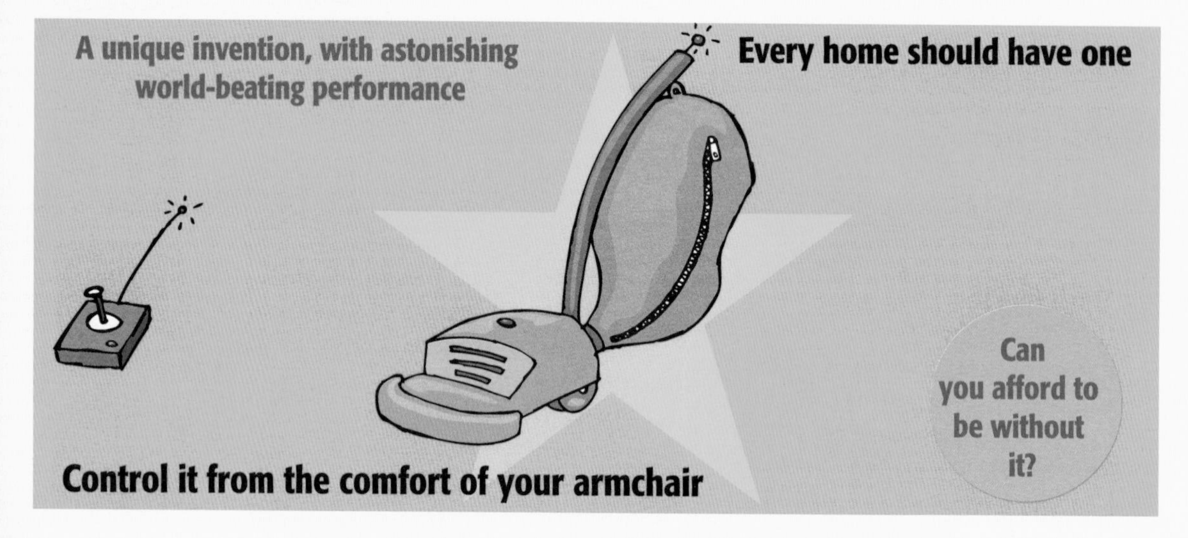

'I know all about advertising techniques,' said Max. 'The written **copy** is designed to **persuade** and they use **emotive** words to help them do this. The **advertising media** also make use of slogans, images, logos and, often, humour to help them sell products. But I do agree that "Every home should have one" – don't you?'

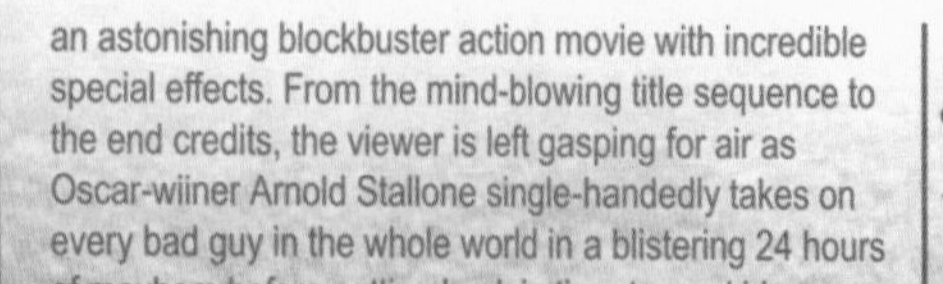

an astonishing blockbuster action movie with incredible special effects. From the mind-blowing title sequence to the end credits, the viewer is left gasping for air as Oscar-wiiner Arnold Stallone single-handedly takes on every bad guy in the whole world in a blistering 24 hours

2 red onions, chopped
3 sun-dried tomatoes, chopped
500g lean minced beef
salt and ground black pepper

to the meat. Cover a
simmer briskly for 5
and cook, stirring oc
until the aubergine i
and it has absorbed

All about advertising

Complete the missing words:

1 All advertisements are designed to _ E _ _ U _ _ _.

2 Advertisers use E _ O _ _ V _ words.

3 Different places where advertisements can appear, such as television, magazine or newspapers, are together called the A _ _ _ R _ _ S _ _ _ M _ _ _ A.

4 Advertising _ _ O _ _ N _ should be short and punchy.

5 The main writing part of an advertisement is called the _ O _ Y and each picture is called an _ M _ _ E.

6 Often advertisements _ E _ L P _ _ D _ _ T _.

7 A special symbol or badge which represents a product or organisation is called a _ _ G _.

8 Many advertisements use H _ _ O _ R to get the audience on their side.

• TOP TIPS •

When analysing advertisements:

- **identify the audience and purpose**
- **look at the visual impact, including the images, headings and captions**
- **examine the ways in which language is used.**

DID YOU KNOW?

The first ever toy product to be advertised on television was Mr Potato Head, which was introduced in 1952. The American TV advert took advantage of the massive viewing power of the millions who had recently bought the newly available TV sets.

Dear Editor,
I was appalled to re[...]n your column abou
the terrible rise in this country of incidents o
antisocial behaviour at village fetes. I mysel

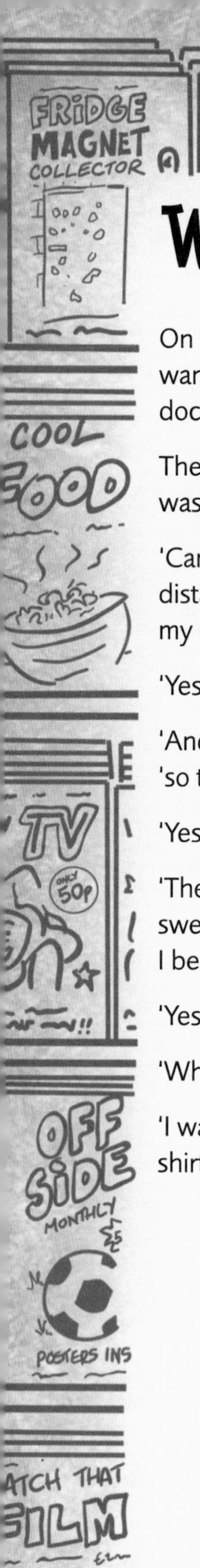

GET INTO KNITTING

My Trip to Asia
by Stephen Cartwright

first arrived in India I was overwhelmed
intense heat. My guide took me to my w
otel, a magnificent 18th century marble

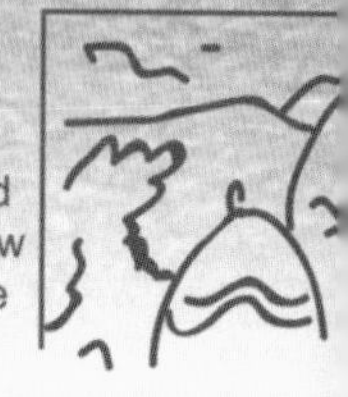

Watch it!

On Wednesday Ralph spent more than his usual two minutes washing and dressing. He wanted to look his best for the arrival of the local TV film crew: they were making a short documentary on his work as an inventor.

The chief cameraman was taken into Ralph's study. Ralph was so excited he hardly let him get a word in edgeways.

'Can you start off with a long shot, showing me at a distance? I could be walking in the grounds, thinking up my next great idea.'

'Yes, Sir Ralph, but –'

'And then move in for a close up,' broke in the inventor, 'so that viewers can see my craggy, handsome face.'

'Yes, Sir Ralph, but –'

'Then you'll need to cut to my workshop, and do a slow, sweeping shot of all the equipment in there – a pan shot, I believe you people call it.'

'Yes, Sir Ralph, but –'

'What is it, man? Let's get shooting!'

'I was just going to point out that you had your shirt on inside out,' said the cameraman.

an astonishing blockbuster action movie with incredible special effects. From the mind-blowing title sequence to the end credits, the viewer is left gasping for air as Oscar-wiiner Arnold Stallone single-handedly takes on every bad guy in the whole world in a blistering 24 hours of mayhem before getting back in time to read his son a

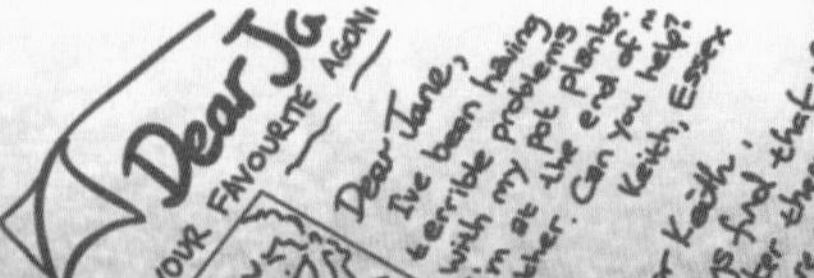

2 red onions, chopped
3 sun-dried tomatoes, chopped
500g lean minced beef
salt and ground black pepper

to the meat. Cover a
simmer briskly for 5
and cook, stirring oc
until the aubergine i
and it has absorbed

Cameraman language

Complete the sentences to find the missing words.

1				C		M				
2						O				
3						V			W	
4						I				
5	C					N				
6				A		G				

7		C				I					
8						M		N			G
9				F		A					
10						G					
11			L			E					

• TOP TIP •

Know the techniques that can be used in film and television and make sure you can use the right words to describe them.

1 You use a __________ to film a scene.

2 The picture the camera takes is called a ______________.

3 Different angles give a different __________ of a scene.

4 Choosing and putting together different camera shots to make a film is called ____________.

5 Choosing actors to play parts is called ________.

6 A camera can take shots from different ________.

7 Changing from one shot to another is called _________.

8 Joining various shots together to create a particular effect is called _________.

9 A single shot in a film is called a ____________.

10 A shot that views the scene from a distance is called a ________ shot.

11 A shot that moves in much closer is called a ___________.

DID YOU KNOW?

In order to create the appearance of the surface of the planet Mars in the film *Mission to Mars* the film crew used a massive sand dune in Canada. They had to cover it in thousands of gallons of red paint to make it exactly the colour they wanted.

Dear Editor,

I was appalled to re[ad] in your column abou[t] the terrible rise in this country of incidents o[f] antisocial behaviour at village fetes. I mysel[f]

Test your knowledge 7

1 What is the difference between a review and a preview?

....

....

(3 marks)

2 List as many things as you can that reviews could be written about.

....

....

....

(5 marks)

3 If you were writing a review of a film or TV programme, name three things that you might comment on.

a) ....

b) ....

c) ....

(6 marks)

4 If you were writing a review of a book, name three things that you might comment on.

a) ....

b) ....

c) ....

(6 marks)

5 In film and television, what do the following terms mean?

a) a long shot ....

b) pan ....

c) editing ....

d) cutting ....

e) frame ....

f) close up ....

(6 marks)

6 In advertising, what do the following terms mean?

a) slogan ....

b) appeal ....

c) consumer reaction ....

d) image ....

(4 marks)

7 List FIVE techniques that might be used in an advertisement.

a) ....

b) ....

c) ....

d) ....

e) ....

(5 marks)

(Total 35 marks)

My Trip to Asia
by Stephen Cartwright

first arrived in India I was overwhelmed
intense heat. My guide took me to my w
otel, a magnificent 18th century marble

Read all about it!

'Izzy,' said Max one morning, 'your dad has made the front page of the local press!'

Izzy grabbed the newspaper that Max was waving in front of her excitedly. 'Oh look at that headline,' she said.

Local Inventor Hits the Big Time

'There's a picture too – it shows Dad in his workshop. He seems to be working on that fold-up bicycle. They must be writing about the success Dad's had in finally persuading the Clever Stuff Company to manufacture his invention.'

'But look at the caption, Izzy.' Max's voice struck a warning note.

'Oh yes, I see what you mean,' said Izzy. '"Mad Professor Strikes Again." Newspapers love an eye-catching headline or caption. I hope the main article doesn't continue the "mad professor" idea.'

'Er, I'm afraid it does,' Max reported with a slight twinkle in his eye!

'Well, it's the amusing human interest stories that sell papers, but I'm not sure that Dad will see the funny side.'

an astonishing blockbuster action movie with incredible special effects. From the mind-blowing title sequence to the end credits, the viewer is left gasping for air as Oscar-wiiner Arnold Stallone single-handedly takes on every bad guy in the whole world in a blistering 24 hours

2 red onions, chopped
3 sun-dried tomatoes, chopped
500g lean minced beef
salt and ground black pepper

to the meat. Cover a
simmer briskly for 5
and cook, stirring oc
until the aubergine i
and it has absorbed

Anatomy of a newspaper

Add labels to the newspaper article below to show that you can identify its main features. (The features are listed in the box on the right.)

ESCAPED PARROT BACK BEHIND BARS

Percy the Parrot's flight for freedom ends

Percy, the African Grey parrot's brief spell of freedom came to an end yesterday when he was re-captured by keepers from Birdland, the park he had escaped from two days earlier. Mrs Hazel Knutt, the park's director said that they were delighted to have Percy back safe and sound and that he had now settled down in the aviary with his fellow parrots. 'He seems none the worse for his adventure,' she commented.

Back in captivity

A tough old bird

He had survived freezing night time temperatures and had been living off nuts put out on bird tables for wild birds. According to experts, although African grey parrots obviously come from a much warmer climate than ours, once they are acclimatised they can survive in very cold conditions.

In fact, some species of parrot that have escaped from aviaries are now living wild in the south of England and have set up breeding colonies.

So next time you think you see a parrot sitting in a tree at the bottom of your garden, look again – it might just be one!

Caption

Image

Sub-heading

Text

Headline

Quotation

SOUN
IRRITATIN

TRAI
BOA
AN
PLA
HOLID

COMPUTER
GAME
EXPERT

DID YOU KNOW?

The oldest continually published newspaper in the world is *Berrow's Worcester Journal.* Established in 1690, it has appeared every week without fail for more than 300 years.

• TOP TIP •

When writing about newspapers, make sure that you use the correct words to describe the features that you are writing about. This will help you say what you want to say – and show that you know what you are talking about!

Dear Editor,

I was appalled to re[ad i]n your column abou the terrible rise in this country of incidents o antisocial behaviour at village fetes. I mysel

My Trip to Asia
by Stephen Cartwright

first arrived in India I was overwhelmed
intense heat. My guide took me to my w
otel, a magnificent 18th century marble

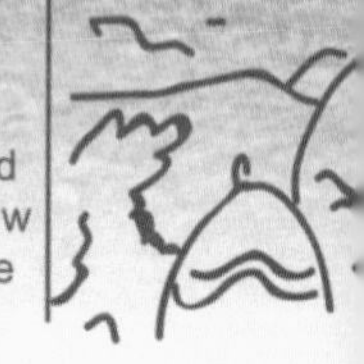

To whom it may concern...

Max and Izzy were sitting watching television one evening when the phone rang.

'I'll get it,' said Izzy. 'I'm expecting a call from Toni. We're all going out tonight.'

Izzy picked up the phone. 'Hi Toni. I thought it might be you. Yeah, yeah. That's right. No! She never did! What? I don't believe it. Yeah, yeah that's OK. Cool. Is that the new place? Claire says it's mint. Yeah. Should be a great night. 'bout six. Text me if you're gonna be late. Bye.'

Just as she sat down, the phone rang again.

'Another of your friends, I expect,' smiled Max.

Izzy picked up the phone up again. 'Hello. Yes, that is correct. This is Isabella speaking. No. I'm afraid that will not be possible. He is out at the moment. Would you like to leave a message, Lady Smythe? Yes. I'll just write this down... He needs to arrive at the Banqueting House no later than 6.30pm and he must make sure that he wears his Chain of Office. Yes. Certainly. I will make absolutely sure that he receives this message. Goodbye, Lady Smythe.'

Max was amused. 'I'm not sure I've witnessed such a swift change from informal to formal language! No-one could accuse you of not knowing when to use the appropriate <u>register</u>.'

COOL FOOD
TV ONLY 50p
OFF SIDE MONTHLY
POSTERS INS
ATCH THAT FILM
RAZY COMIC

an astonishing blockbuster action movie with incredible special effects. From the mind-blowing title sequence to the end credits, the viewer is left gasping for air as Oscar-wiiner Arnold Stallone single-handedly takes on every bad guy in the whole world in a blistering 24 hours

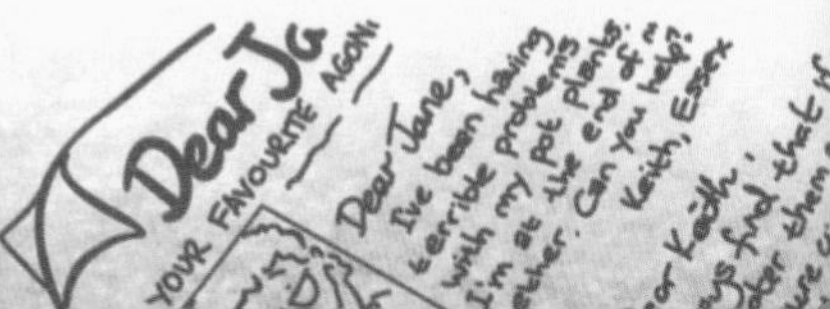

2 red onions, chopped
3 sun-dried tomatoes, chopped
500g lean minced beef
salt and ground black pepper

to the meat. Cover a
simmer briskly for 5
and cook, stirring oc
until the aubergine i
and it has absorbed

Formal or informal?

In the box below there are ten occasions when **formal** language should be used, and six when **informal** language is acceptable. Highlight them in two different colours.

• TOP TIP •

Remember that formal language pays close attention to the rules of grammar. It avoids slang, colloquialisms and contractions, such as 'can't'. Sentence structure and vocabulary are often more complex.

DID YOU KNOW?

If you are writing to the Queen you should begin your letter either 'Madam' or 'May it please your Majesty'. Your letter should end, 'I have the honour to remain Madam, Your Majesty's most humble and obedient servant.' If you are speaking with the Queen you should address her as 'Your Majesty' to begin with and then 'Ma'am' (pronounced to rhyme with 'Pam') after that.

Dear Editor,
I was appalled to re... in your column abou
the terrible rise in this country of incidents o
antisocial behaviour at village fetes. I mysel

My Trip to Asia
by Stephen Cartwright

first arrived in India I was overwhelmed
intense heat. My guide took me to my w
otel, a magnificent 18th century marble

Post bag

Ralph was in despair. He was looking forward to reading the morning post, but Spotless had got to the mat before him and run off with the letters. When Izzy eventually tracked down the dog it was too late – the letters were all ripped in pieces.

'Never mind, Dad,' she said, standing in front of Spotless to protect him from his master's wrath. 'I'll help you put them back together again.'

It was quite a jigsaw puzzle, but they managed. What helped was spotting whether a letter was formal or informal. Those written in formal language usually came from businesses or organisations. They not only had the name and address of the business at the top, but also included Ralph's name and address on the left.

Ralph knew that letters that began

Dear Ralph

ended

Yours sincerely

whereas those that simply began

Dear Sir or Madam

always ended

Yours faithfully.

After two hours they had completed the jigsaw. Only one 'piece' was missing – a tartan kilt sent to Ralph by his Scottish cousin.

an astonishing blockbuster action movie with incredible special effects. From the mind-blowing title sequence to the end credits, the viewer is left gasping for air as Oscar-wiiner Arnold Stallone single-handedly takes on every bad guy in the whole world in a blistering 24 hours

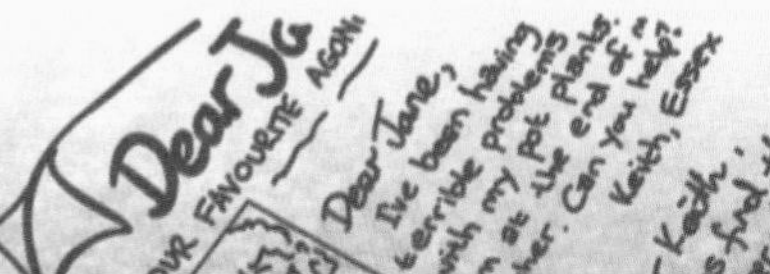

2 red onions, chopped
3 sun-dried tomatoes, chopped
500g lean minced beef
alt and ground black pepper

to the meat. Cover a
simmer briskly for 5
and cook, stirring oc
until the aubergine i
and it has absorbed

Letter perfect

Read the following letter and identify EIGHT things that are wrong with it.

Rowan Street
Newtell
West Yorkshire

Dear Sir

I am writing to you to complain about something I bought recently. The problem is that it doesn't work properly and I would be grateful if you would let me know what you can do about it

Yours sincerely

Jane Smith

DID YOU KNOW?

In 2004, to mark the 125th anniversary of Bolivia's loss of land to its neighbour Chile, school children were involved in a project to produce the world's longest letter. Thousands of children's letters, addressed to the United Nations, were stapled together to create a single letter more than 130 km long.

• TOP TIPS •

When writing a letter:

- **make sure that you lay it out correctly**
- **end with the correct phrase to match the way you have started your letter**
- **use formal or informal language consistently throughout, depending which is appropriate to your purpose.**

Dear Editor,
I was appalled to re[ad] in your column abou[t]
the terrible rise in this country of incidents o[f]
antisocial behaviour at village fetes. I mysel[f]

Test your knowledge 8

1 Make a list of FIVE different kinds of news that you often find in a newspaper.

a) ....

b) ....

c) ....

d) ....

e) ....

(5 marks)

2 Briefly explain what the following features of a newspaper report are:

a) headline

....

....

b) image

....

....

c) caption

....

....

d) fact

....

....

e) opinion

....

....

(10 marks)

3 In which of these spoken situations would you use FORMAL language?

a) a conversation with a friend

b) an interview with your headteacher

c) a chat with your mum

d) a speech to your class

e) reading a radio news bulletin as part of your oral work in English

f) taking part in a formal debate

g) talking to a relative on the telephone

(7 marks)

4 In which of these written contexts would you use FORMAL language?

a) a holiday postcard to a friend

b) a letter of complaint to a company

c) a letter to a penfriend abroad

d) a report on a science experiment

e) a discussion essay written in your English lesson

f) a note of thanks to a relative for a present s/he has sent you

g) a text message

(7 marks)

5 Underline the correct answer in each case.

a) If you begin your letter 'Dear Sir' or Dear Madam', you should end it 'Yours (sincerely, faithfully, truly)'.

b) Your address should go at the (top, centre, bottom) of your letter.

c) Your letter should always give (the date, the place, the time) it was written.

d) You might write an informal letter to (a newspaper, the prime minister, a friend).

e) A letter of application for a job is an example of a (formal, informal) letter.

f) If you begin a letter 'Dear Miss Andrews', you should end it ('Yours faithfully', 'Yours sincerely', 'Your friend').

(6 marks)

(Total 35 marks)

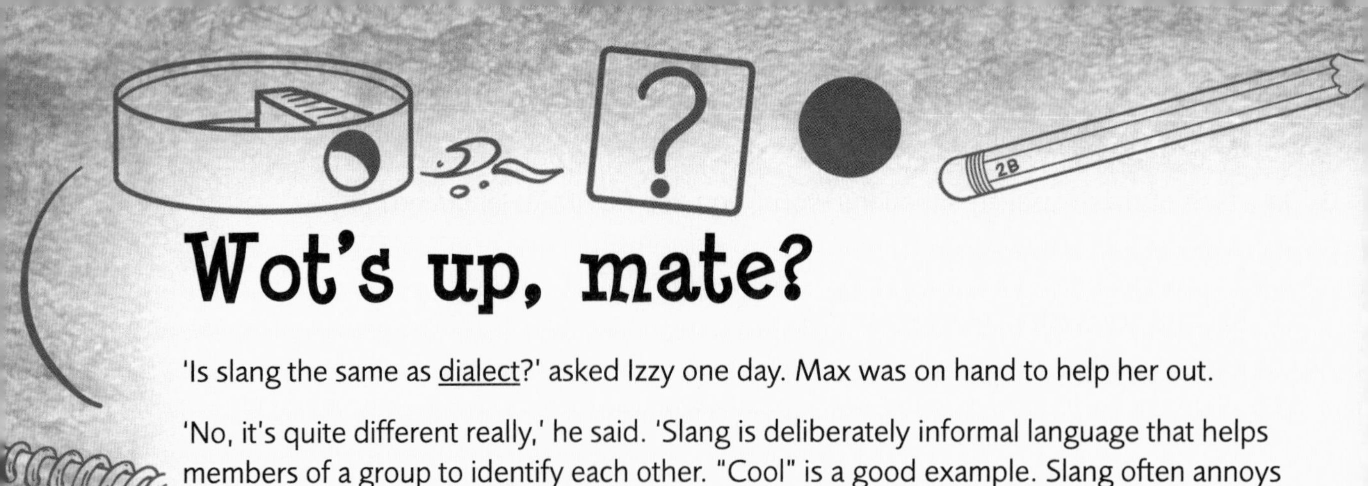

Wot's up, mate?

'Is slang the same as dialect?' asked Izzy one day. Max was on hand to help her out.

'No, it's quite different really,' he said. 'Slang is deliberately informal language that helps members of a group to identify each other. "Cool" is a good example. Slang often annoys people in authority, such as teachers –'

'And parents,' broke in Izzy ruefully.

'And parents,' agreed Max. 'Dialect, on the other hand, is a different form of the language often linked to a particular region of the country. Sometimes it involves special words, but it can have its own grammar too. I remember once when I was in Yorkshire I got chatting to a man and asked him if there was anywhere to get a bite to eat and a drink. He said to me,

> **"Not half. Yer just slip down th' ginnel theer and tha'll see a caf. Thi du good jock theer – tha'll get a smashing barm cake. Theer's a gud pub nixt doar an all where thi can get a gill to wesh it dahn wi."'**

'That sounded pretty cool, but I didn't get half of it!' said Izzy.

'I managed to figure it out in the end,' said Max.

Where does it come from?

Draw a line to match the dialect word (on the left) to the correct definition (on the right). Four of them are from the North of England and four from the South. Use a wavy line for the Northern words, and a straight line for the Southern words.

Jiggered	ran away
Bairn	small child
Brass	house or place
Littly	money
Had it away on his toes	tired
Gaff	phone
Wonga	child
Dog	money

• TOP TIPS •

Don't confuse slang and dialect:

- **Slang is a word or phrase in deliberately non-Standard English, used by a particular group (e.g. teenagers) and often to show that you belong to that group.**
- **Dialect is a language variety used in a particular region, which differs from Standard English in vocabulary and/or grammar.**
- **Accent is different still – it means the way a word is pronounced, e.g. the word 'bath' is pronounced 'barth' in the South of England.**

DID YOU KNOW?

'OK' is the most successful and widespread of all American slang terms. It is known and used worldwide by many nations and is universally understood in almost any language. It was also the fourth word spoken on the surface of the moon. It stands for 'oll korrect', a misspelling of 'all correct'.

Check it out

Despite trying to get rid of Julian, her admirer, by handing back his love poem with a written commentary, Izzy was still the subject of his unending love and attention. This was driving her to distraction.

'Why won't he take no for an answer?' she said to Max one day after school. 'What do I have to do, put it in writing?'

'Perhaps that would be a very good idea,' said Max.

Izzy sat down at her desk and got straight to work. She wanted so desperately to be rid of this boy that she hardly glanced at what she had written. As she swept downstairs to put the note in her schoolbag, Max grabbed it.

'I hope that you've checked your work thoroughly,' he said with a smile. 'It might be quite important. Hmmm ... looks like Julian is going to be pleasantly surprised.' And he showed Izzy what she had written:

Dear Julian

Will you please let me be

yours

Isabella

Izzy was horrified. She raced back to her room and paid much more attention to her second draft:

Dear Julian

Will you please let me be?

yours

Isabella

'That was close!' she thought, as she put the note in her bag. 'I suddenly see why our teachers are always on about **drafting** and **editing** our work!'

Drafting puzzle

All the words in this puzzle are to do with drafting and editing your work.

1						E	D						
2						G	R						
3					R		A						
4				D			F						
5			P				T						
6		Q					I						
7	S						N						
8	W						G						

1 Checking your work, and cutting out and changing bits of it is called ....

2 You should read your work through and check your ....

3 To get everything right it is important to .... your work carefully.

4 The first copy of your work is called your first ....

5 Check capital letters, commas and other ....

6 Your work should answer the ....

7 You should check your .... carefully.

8 Make sure that your .... is clear and neat.

TOP TIP

Teachers and examiners will give you credit for editing your work, which shows you know how it can be improved.

DID YOU KNOW?

In 1796, when Jane Austen was 21, she wrote the novel *First Impressions.* Seventeen years later, she re-drafted the work and re-named it *Pride and Prejudice.* It became her best known and perhaps greatest novel.

Point taken!

Ralph and Max had to go out. Ralph was expecting several important telephone calls, so he asked Izzy to answer the phone and note down all the details of each call.

'What exactly do you want me to note down, Dad?' asked Izzy carelessly.

'Well, there are three key things I need to know,' replied her father, writing them down.

- First of all, the name of the person who rang
- secondly, what the message is
- and thirdly a number I can get back to them on.

'Right. I think I've got that – brief but to the point, containing the essential information clearly. Leave it to me – no worries.'

Ten minutes later the phone rang. Izzy picked it up.

'Oh, Izzy,' came her father's voice. 'Could you feed Spotless? I forgot this morning.'

'Let me just write this down,' said Izzy mischievously. 'Your name, please?'

Taking notes on... Rupert Grint

Try making notes on this article about Rupert Grint (the actor who plays Ron Weasley in the Harry Potter films). Can you condense all the key facts into four or five short bullet points?

Rupert Grint *Actor*

Rupert had only done the odd bit of drama at school when, on Newsround, he saw a request for young actors that were wanted for a Harry Potter movie. He put together a video of himself acting and rapping about playing Ron Weasley. At 11 he landed his first film role. He is currently shooting the fourth in the series, Harry Potter And The Goblet Of Fire. In between Potters, he appeared in Thunderpants with Simon Callow and Stephen Fry, and recently recorded the voice of Peter Pan for a BBC documentary to mark the book's centenary.

• TOP TIPS •

- **Make sure that your notes contain only the key points of information – not too much detail.**
- **It is a good idea to write down where you got the notes from (i.e. which book, magazine etc.) so that you can go back to the original source later to look up any extra information you might want.**

DID YOU KNOW?

- **We forget 50% of what we hear immediately and two months later we have forgotten another 25%.**
- **Research conducted on students found that facts that were noted down were six times more likely to be remembered than facts that were not written down.**

Test your knowledge 9

1 What kind of language are you using if you use SLANG?

....

(1 mark)

2 Jargon is a particular kind of slang. Can you describe in more detail what it is?

....

(3 marks)

3 Explain the meaning of the following 'slang' words.

a) grub ....

b) nick ....

c) pal ....

d) con ....

e) scram ....

(10 marks)

4 What is meant by ACCENT?

....

(3 marks)

5 If you edit a piece of your work what do you do with it?

....

(2 marks)

6 If you check through your work, correct any errors and write it out again, what is this called?

....

(2 marks)

7 Check the following pieces of writing and redraft them correctly:

> their has been alot of debate resently on the topic of fox hunting but the subject still dose not seem to be decide becorse it is not clear what is going on in the future.

> i ran as fast as i can and arrived five minuets late for the apoinmtent but it didnt matter because the teecher was late because she ha to go to a meeting that ended late.

(10 marks)

8 Complete the sentences:

a) When making notes you should write down the .... points.

b) Your notes should be .... and easy to understand.

c) You should not include unnecessary ....

d) In order to present key points clearly you might use .... points.

(4 marks)

(Total 35 marks)

Glossary

Abstract noun
A noun that names something intangible, such as an idea or feeling, e.g. love, fear.

Adjective
A word that describes a noun, e.g. 'the red balloon'.

Adverb
A word that tells you more about a verb, e.g. 'he ran quickly'.

Advert
A poster or feature in a magazine, newspaper or on television etc. that tries to persuade the audience to do something, e.g. to buy or believe something.

Advertising techniques
Particular language, visual or sound techniques that advertisers use to make their adverts more effective.

Alliteration
The repetition of the same consonant sounds, e.g. 'silky smooth soft hair'. This is a technique often used in advertising and poetry, among other forms of writing.

Assonance
The repetition of vowel sounds in words, e.g. 'though the dough'.

Atmosphere
The feeling often associated with a sense of place.

Audience
The target group of readers or viewers that a text or programme is aimed at.

Autobiography
A life story written by the person him/herself.

Ballad
A poem that tells a story, often originally set to music.

Blank verse
Unrhymed poetry with a regular ten syllables in each line.

Caption
A short text that goes with a photograph or picture.

Characters
Fictitious people in plays and stories.

Close up
In film, TV or photography, a picture taken close to the subject.

Comedy
A play that is often amusing and ends happily.

Common noun
A noun that names an everyday object, e.g. table, door, road.

Cut
In film or TV, to move quickly from one shot to another.

Dialect
A language variety used in a particular region, which differs from Standard English in vocabulary and/or grammar.

Dialogue
Speech or conversation.

Elegy
A poem, often sad in tone, concerned with the theme of death.

Emotive
Language is described as emotive when it is designed to make the audience feel something.

Fiction
Literature that describes imaginary events and people.

First person
A poem or story is in the first person if it is told by the writer using 'I', e.g. 'I had worried all day'.

Frame
In film or TV, an individual picture.

Free verse
Verse that has no fixed structure in terms of rhyme, rhythm, form etc.

Haiku
A short poem consisting of three lines of five, then seven, then five syllables.

Image
In advertising, newspapers etc., a picture, illustration or photograph; in writing, a picture created through words.

Jargon
A kind of slang or technical language used by a specific group of people, e.g. soldiers, doctors, scientists.

Long shot
In film or TV, a shot taken from a distance.

Metaphor
A comparison of one thing to another in order to make a vivid description. Unlike a simile, it does not use the words 'like' or 'as'.

Montage
Joining together various shots to create a particular effect.

Narrative
A story, e.g. a narrative poem is one that tells a story.

Newspaper
A daily, weekly or Sunday periodical that reports news of many kinds.

Non-fiction
Writing that deals with things that are true.

Noun
A word that names an object or quality, e.g. 'window'.

Novel
A long, fictitious story published as a book.

Ode
A type of poem that often deals with serious or philosophical ideas.

Onomatopoeia
The use of words whose sounds copy the sound of the thing they describe, e.g. 'bang'.

Pamphlet
A small booklet.

Personification
Writing about something that is not a living thing as if it were living, had feelings etc.

Persuade
To encourage someone to do something or think something or act in a particular way.

Plot
The storyline of a play or novel.

Proper noun
A noun that names a specific person, place or thing, e.g. London, Andrew.

Prose
Any kind of writing that is not verse – usually divided into fiction and non-fiction.

Purpose
The effect that a text is designed to have.

Register
The level of formality of language used, e.g. informal or formal.

Review
A piece of writing that gives an opinion on a particular subject, e.g. a book or a film.

Rhetorical question
A technique that uses questions for effect rather than to want an answer.

Rhyme
Corresponding sounds in words, usually at the end of each line of poetry.

Rhythm
The 'beat' or sense of movement in a poem created through the stresses in the words.

Scene
The sections that plays are often divided into.

Sentence
A group of words that usually makes complete sense in itself and contains a subject, object and verb.

Setting
The place or environment that a story, play, film etc. is set in.

Shot
In film, TV or photography, a specific picture of the subject.

Simile
A comparison of one thing to another to create a vivid description, usually using the words 'like' or 'as'.

Slang
Particular informal words or phrases often used by specific groups, such as teenagers.

Slogan
A catchy phrase used in advertising, designed to catch the attention.

Soliloquy
A speech in a play spoken by a character alone on the stage – usually used to let the audience know what is in the character's mind.

Sonnet
A 14-line poem, usually with ten syllables in each line.

Stage directions
Short instructions in a play telling the actors how to move, look etc.

Stanza
Blocks of lines that poems are sometimes arranged in.

Theme
The ideas that a story, play, film etc. explores.

Third person
A poem or story is in the third person if the narrator is not one of the characters, e.g. 'He did this', 'She did that'.

Tragedy
A play or novel with a sad ending, usually the death of the main character and sometimes that of several other characters.

Verb
A word that describes an action e.g. 'to run'.

Viewpoint
The point of view that a story or poem is told from.

Vocabulary
The words that are used in a piece of writing.

Voice-over
In TV advertisements or documentaries, when a commentary accompanies the pictures on the screen.

Answers

Out of order (p7)

1 I am writing to you about my idea for a collapsible bicycle.
2 There are several reasons why this is a useful invention.
3 First, by encouraging people to cycle, we are helping the health of the nation.
4 Secondly, if more people cycle, pollution will be reduced.
5 In addition, this cycle is so light and easy to fold away that it can be carried in a sports bag.
6 This fact will encourage people to use it to get to work or the shops, not just for recreation.
7 I would be grateful if you would consider these obvious benefits, and think about manufacturing and selling the bicycle.
8 Please contact me if you require any further information.

Persuasive crossword (p9)

Across: 1 persuasive, 3 personal, 5 rhetorical, 9 emotive, 10 reasons, 11 ideas
Down: 2 repetition, 4 points, 6 humour, 7 adverbs, 8 tone

Advise, inform or explain? (p13)

Advise = 1, 6, 8; inform = 4, 5, 9; explain = 2, 3, 7, 10

Where's that word? (p15)

1 Fiction, 2 Adjective, 3 Novel, 4 Adverb, 5 Vocabulary, 6 Mystery, 7 Fantasy, 8 Action, 9 Narrative, 10 Short story

Complete the spiral (p17)

1 run, 2 number, 3 right, 4 taste, 5 ears, 6 seat, 7 trip, 8 play, 9 yacht, 10 tango, 11 orange, 12 eat, 13 tent, 14 think, 15 kilogram, 16 move

All about characters (p21)

1 actions, 2 thinks, 3 behave, 4 description, 5 dialogue, 6 convincing, 7 relationships, 8 language, 9 created, 10 say

What a feeling (p23)

1 frightening, 2 happy, 3 creepy, 4 tense, 5 mysterious

Transformations (p25)

loveable, pleasant, explosive, quarrelsome, sympathetic, hopeful, foolish, childlike, sandy, heroic, musical, friendly

All about poetry (p29)

Across: 4 aloud, 5 content, 6 read, 8 atmosphere, 10 theme, 11 Armitage
Down: 1 third, 2 poet, 3 language, 5 crow, 7 effects, 9 Owen

Types of poem (p31)

1 sonnet, 2 limerick, 3 ballad, 4 haiku, 5 free verse, 6 stanza, 7 ode, 8 rhythm, 9 elegy, 10 line

Making it rhyme (p33)

cloud, hills, crowd, daffodils, trees, breeze, shine, way, line, bay, glance, dance

Use the right term (p39)

alliteration = 1, 5; assonance = 2, 7, 8; onomatopoeia = 3, 4, 6

Word snake (p41)

1 night, 2 tide, 3 echo, 4 orange, 5 earth, 6 horse, 7 eel, 8 light, 9 tower, 10 red, 11 dust, 12 tree

Playscript puzzle (p47)

1 opening, 2 plot, 3 stage, 4 say, 5 speeches, 6 characters, 7 props, 8 climax, 9 speech marks, 10 tension

How to write your autobiography (p49)
first person narration, chronological order, chapter, planned it carefully, notes

Which review? (p53)

1 film, 2 computer game, 3 novel, 4 CD, 5 play

All about advertising (p55)

1 persuade, 2 emotive, 3 advertising media, 4 slogans, 5 copy, image, 6 sell products, 7 logo, 8 humour

Cameraman language (p57)

1 camera, 2 shot, 3 view, 4 editing, 5 casting, 6 angles, 7 cutting, 8 montage, 9 frame, 10, long, 11 close up

Formal or informal? (p63)

Formal: letter to a newspaper, interview, school report, police statement, job application, broadsheet newspaper article, examination, wedding speech, sermon, BBC news summary
Informal: email, note to milkman, text message, advertisement, playground conversation, pop song

Letter perfect (p65)

House number missing on address; no postcode; no date; business address missing; the letter does not state: what item had been bought, what is wrong with the item, where the item had been bought from; the letter ends Yours sincerely instead of Yours faithfully

Where does it come from? (p69)

Jiggered – tired (Lancashire)
Bairn – child (North East)
Brass – money (Lancashire and Yorkshire)
Littly – small child (Liverpool)
Had it away on his toes – ran away (London and South East)
Gaff – house or place (London and South East)
Wonga – money (London and South East)
Dog – phone (Cockney rhyming slang, 'dog and bone')

Drafting puzzle (p71)

1 editing, 2 grammar, 3 read, 4 draft, 5 punctuation, 6 question, 7 spelling, 8 writing

Taking notes on... Rupert Grint (p73)

Put together a video of himself acting Ron Weasley to win 1st film role at 11
Now shooting 4th Harry Potter film
Appeared in Thunderpants
Recently was voice of Peter Pan in BBC documentary

Test your knowledge 1

1 (select from) report; advert; poem; novel; play; short story; newspaper article; brochure; information leaflet; instructions
2 a) writing that is not true – it is made up from the imagination
  b) writing that deals with things that are true
3 fiction – novel; play; short story; narrative poem
  non-fiction – football report; biography; history text book; newspaper report
4 a) giving one side of the argument or one view of a particular issue
  b) language that appeals to the emotions (often to try to persuade the reader)
  c) a question that does not require an answer – often used to create a persuasive effect in speech and writing
5 fact – something that is true
  opinion – someone's own view on something
6 fact – b, e, g, h
  opinion – a, c, d, f
7 to make a point more effectively
8 (select from) advert; political pamphlet; charity leaflet; newspaper report

Test your knowledge 2

1 (possible answers) a road safety leaflet; a pamphlet on choosing your subject options; a booklet giving advice on healthy eating; a report on using mobile phones safely; a leaflet on road safety
2 a) clear, concise, b) sections, c) bullet, d) audience, purpose
3 plot, characters, setting
4 capture the reader's attention
5 the storyline
6 the place where the story takes place
7 what they say, what they do, what other characters say about them
8 a word that names something
9 proper nouns: Kieran, Wednesday, Manchester;
  common nouns: compact disc, skin, hammer;
  abstract nouns: fashion, weight, joke

Test your knowledge 3

1 vivid description; convincing speech; believable actions.
2 a) speech, b) speech marks (inverted commas), c) third-person, d) first-person
3 a) where a story is set
  b) the particular 'feeling' associated with a place
4 a) a word that describes a noun
  b) bright; yellow; whole; blue; cloudless; wonderful
5 a) circular, b) troublesome, c) gigantic, d) parental
6 a) a word that describes a verb
  b) quickly; loudly; suddenly; broadly
  c) hungrily, lazily, loudly, quietly, cheekily

Test your knowledge 4

1 a) corresponding sounds in words, usually at the end of each line
  b) the 'beat' of a poem
  c) no
2 a) 14, b) blocks of lines that a poem can be divided into
3 haiku
4 a narrative poem
5 a ballad
6 limerick
7 a) 8, b) 8, c) 8, d) 7, e) 6

Test your knowledge 5

1 a comparison of one thing to another to create a vivid description (usually uses the words 'like' or 'as')
2 a comparison of one thing to another by saying that one thing *is* another
3 a) bone, b) lead, c) feather, d) whistle, e) sheet, f) fox
4 a word that sounds like the sound it describes
5 (possible answers) bang; clang; clash; hiss; crack; thud
6 a) personification, b) alliteration, c) metaphor, d) simile
7 cobbles he clattered and clashed – alliteration
  clattered and clashed – onomatopoeia
  there/hair – rhyme
  creaked/peaked – rhyme

His eyes were hollows of madness – metaphor
his hair like mouldy hay – simile
Dumb as a dog he listened – simile

Test your knowledge 6

1 it needs to capture the audience's interest and attention
2 a play with an unhappy ending – usually resulting in the death of one or more of the characters
3 a play that ends happily and often contains amusing or funny incidents and characters
4 (choose from) Romeo and Juliet; Macbeth; A Midsummer Night's Dream; Twelfth Night; The Tempest; Othello; Much Ado About Nothing; Julius Caesar
5 The Globe
6 a) a speech spoken by a character alone on the stage
   b) a fictitious person in a play
   c) the instructions in a play telling the actors how to move, how to speak the lines, what the scene is like etc.
   d) the sections that a play is divided up into
   e) lines spoken by a character in a play meant to be heard by the audience but not the other characters on stage
   f) the items that actors use in the play, e.g. swords, goblets
   g) the lines spoken by actors in a play
   h) the way the action of the play is put together
   i) the ideas that a play explores
   j) a production of a play
   k) a character played by an actor in a play
   l) where the action of a play is meant to take place
7 No
8 a) verse: regular rhythm, set out in lines
   b) prose: no regular rhythm and set out as continuous text
9 a) A biography is a book written by someone about the life of someone else; an autobiography is a person's account of their own life.
10 a) third person, b) first person
11 diary
12 it recounts the experiences of a Jewish girl in hiding from the Nazis during the Second World War

Test your knowledge 7

1 A review gives information about a film, TV programme or book etc. that has been released or screened; a preview gives information about a film, TV programme or book etc. that has not yet been released or screened.
2 (possible answers) novels; TV programmes; films; computer games; computers; stereo systems; CDs
3 (choose from) the acting, the setting, special effects, storyline, script
4 (choose from) the storyline (plot), how effectively the characters are drawn, the quality of the description, language used, the themes and ideas explored
5 a) a shot showing the scene/characters from a distance
   b) the camera moving to follow a particular object or show more of the scene
   c) to prepare a film by rearranging, cutting and moving material
   d) to move from one shot to another
   e) an individual picture
   f) a picture taken close to the subject
6 a) a catchy phrase (often used in advertising)
   b) in advertising, something designed to be attractive to the target audience
   c) how the potential buyers of a product react to it or the advertising of it
   d) a picture or photograph (often used as part of an advert)
7 (choose from) alliteration; exaggeration; images; emotive language; repetition; rhetorical questions; plays on words; specialised language

Test your knowledge 8

1 (choose from) international news; home news; local news; sports news; soaps news; film and TV news; political news; financial news
2 a) the main title above a story
   b) a picture
   c) a title or brief explanation that goes with an image
   d) something that has actually happened, or that is the case
   e) what someone thinks about something
3 b, d, e, f
4 b, d, e, f
5 a) faithfully, b) top, c) date, d) a friend, e) formal, f) Yours sincerely

Test your knowledge 9

1 informal use of words or phrases
2 a specific kind of slang often used to describe technical language or the language used by a particular group, e.g. soldiers, doctors
3 Food, steal, friend, trick, run away
4 the way a word is pronounced – often determined by the part of the country the speaker comes from
5 cut things out, re-arrange parts of it to create the effect you want
6 redrafting
7 a) There has been a lot of debate recently on the topic of fox hunting but the subject still does not seem to have been decided because it is not clear what is going to happen in the future.
   b) I ran as fast as I could and arrived five minutes late for the appointment. It didn't matter, though, as the teacher was late too, because she had been at a meeting that had ended late.
8 a) key, b) concise, c) detail (or information), d) bullet